Medical Humor

Medical Nonsense to Tickle Your Funnybone

Thomas F. Shubnell, Ph.D.

ISBN 1440415749

Cover and interior design by TFS

If you enjoy this, you will also love, "Gracious Me . . . Is Nothing Sacred." A non-sectarian and hilarious look at all religions from the beginning of time. It truly proves that laughter is good for the soul.

Another wacky book, "Men vs. Women, a Book of Lists" examines life from a different perspective and tells it all - the differences between the sexes are real and funny.

Even more fun can be found in "The Best of Terrible Tommy and Yucky Chucky," a collection of the best Terrible Tommy and Yucky Chucky jokes of all time.

More hilarious reading can be found in "Giggles, Gags, and Quips Special Picks" a collection of the best jokes, pictures, billboards, stories, and cartoons.

Also collect all the rest of the "Greatest Jokes of the Century" series of books. They are wildly funny and hilarious compendiums of the greatest jokes, tidbits, stories, and trivia that are sure to induce uncontrollable laughter. The best bathroom reading since Readers Digest.

All written by Thomas F. Shubnell and available at

Amazon.com

Table of Contents

History of Medicine

"Doctor, I have a problem."

2000 B.C. - "Here, eat this root."

1000 B.C. - "That root is heathen, say this prayer."

1850 A.D. - "That prayer is superstition, drink this potion."

1940 A.D. - "That potion is snake oil, swallow this pill."

1980 A.D. - "That pill is ineffective, take this antibiotic."

2000 A.D. - "That antibiotic is artificial. Here, eat this root."

Bless physicians and nurses.
Give them wisdom, skill, sympathy,
and patients.

OFFICE VISITS

OFFICE FINDINGS

The doctor says to her patient "Mr. Beck, I'm afraid you are not quite as sick as we had hoped."

A man went to see his physician because of being constipated and was given a number of suppositories. Unfortunately, he lost the instructions that had been provided, and was too embarrassed to call his doctor for the directions.

Five days later, the doctor received an angry call, "Doctor, I don't know how you got that job, but for all the good these pills are doing, I might as well stick them up my butt."

The doctor said to reduce my stress, so I handed his bill back to him.

Why do doctors leave the room while you change?
They are going to see you naked anyway.

Doctor: I'm afraid you have a dodgy ticker.

Patient: Thank goodness. I was afraid there might be something wrong with my heart.

"Doc, I can't stop singing, 'The green, green grass of home'."

"That sounds like Tom Jones syndrome."

"Is it common?"

"It's not unusual."

A patient was waiting nervously in the examination room of a famous specialist.

"Who did you see before coming to me?" asked the doctor.

"My local General Practitioner."

"Your GP?" scoffed the doctor. "What a waste of time. Tell me, what sort of useless advice did he give you?"

"He told me to come and see you."

Doctor, doctor will this ointment clear up my spots?

I never make rash promises.

I think we found your problem, Mr. Addy. Too much fiber.

Each year, the Maryland Trial Lawyers Association plays a baseball game against the Maryland Physician's baseball team. One year, the Physician's team easily defeated the Trial Lawyers team.

The trial lawyers, in their usual positive manner posted the following announcement, "The Maryland Trial Lawyers Association is pleased to announce that for the current baseball season, we came in second place since we only lost one game this year. The Maryland Physicians had a poor year, and only won one game."

Doctor: Did that medicine I gave your uncle straighten him out?
Patient: Certainly did. They buried him yesterday.

Life is sexually transmitted.

A man walks into a doctor's office. He has a cucumber up his nose, a carrot in his left ear and a banana in his right ear.
"What's the matter with me?" he asks the doctor.
The doctor replies, "You're not eating properly."

After his annual physical, a sexually active bachelor was waiting in the doctor's office for the results. The doctor said, "I have good news and bad news for you."
"The way I feel, please give me the good news first," replied the bachelor.
"The good news is that your penis has grown an additional four inches since your last exam."
"Great," the man shouted, "What is the bad news?"
"It's malignant," replied the doctor.

Constipated people just don't give a crap.

"I came in to make an appointment with the dentist." said a man to the receptionist."
"I'm sorry sir." she replied. "He's out right now, but. . ."
"Thank you," interrupted the patient. "When will he be out again?"

A construction worker goes to the doctor and says, "Doc, I'm constipated."

The doctor examines him for a minute and then says, "Lean over the table." The construction worker leans over the table, the doctor whacks him on the ass with a baseball bat, and then sends him into the bathroom.

He comes out a few minutes later and says, "Doc, I feel great. What should I do next?"

The doctor says, "Stop wiping with cement bags."

Doctor, doctor I keep thinking I'm a frog.
So what's wrong with that?
I think I'm going to croak.

There was a young dentist named Sloan
Who catered to women alone.
In an act of depravity,
He filled the wrong cavity,
And said, "My, how my business has grown."

Last week I went to the doctor and he gave me a pain reliever.
It didn't work. When I got home, my wife was still there.

Never accept a drink from a Urologist.

A man walked into his doctor's office and complained that he had a huge erection lasting seven days.

The nurse took him into the examining room and told him to disrobe and lie on the table.

The doctor came in, looked at the man's erection, and saw a huge fly on the head of the man's penis.

The doctor flicked off the fly and the man's erection immediately went down.

The man exclaimed, "What a relief, how much do I owe you?"

"Nothing, if I can catch that fly."

A streetwalker was visiting her doctor for a regular checkup.

“Any specific problems you want to tell me about?” the doctor asked.

“I have noticed lately that if I get even the tiniest cut anywhere on my body, it seems to bleed for hours,” she replied. “Do you think I might be a hemophiliac?”

The doctor answered, “Hemophilia is a genetic disorder and it is more often found in men, but it is possible for a woman to be a hemophiliac. Tell me, how much you lose when you have your period?”

After calculating for a moment the woman replied, “About a thousand dollars, I think.”

“Doctor, doctor, my leg hurts, what shall I do?”
“Limp.”

Why did the guru refuse Novocain when he went to his dentist?
He wanted to transcend dental medication.

The only man who can tell a woman when to open and when to shut her mouth, and get away with it, is a dentist.

A man came home from the doctor looking very worried. His wife asked, "What's the problem?"

"The doctor told me I have to take a pill every day for the rest of my life," he said.

"So what?" she replied. "Lots of people have to take a pill every day their lives."

He said, "I know, but he only gave me four pills."

"Doctor, doctor, my hair is coming out. Can you give me something to keep it in?"
"Certainly, how about a paper bag?"

Two children are in a doctor's waiting room, and one of them is crying.

"Why are you crying?" asked the other child.

"I'm here for a blood test, and they are going to cut my finger."

The other child began to cry.

"Why are you crying?"

"I'm here for a urine test."

Dentist: There goes the only woman I ever loved.
Assistant: Why don't you marry her?
Dentist: I can't afford to. She's my best patient.

When a physician remarked on a new patient's extraordinarily ruddy complexion, he said, "High blood pressure, doc. It runs in the family."

"Your mother's side or your father's?" the doctor asked.

"Neither," he replied. "It's from my wife's family."

"I don't understand," the doctor said, "How could your wife's family give you high blood pressure?"

The man sighed, "You should meet them sometime, doc."

Giving a man his physical, a doctor noticed several dark, ugly bruises on his shins, so he asked, "Do you play hockey?"
"No"
"Do you play soccer?"
"No"
"Do you play any other physical sport?"
"Not at all. I just play bridge with my wife."

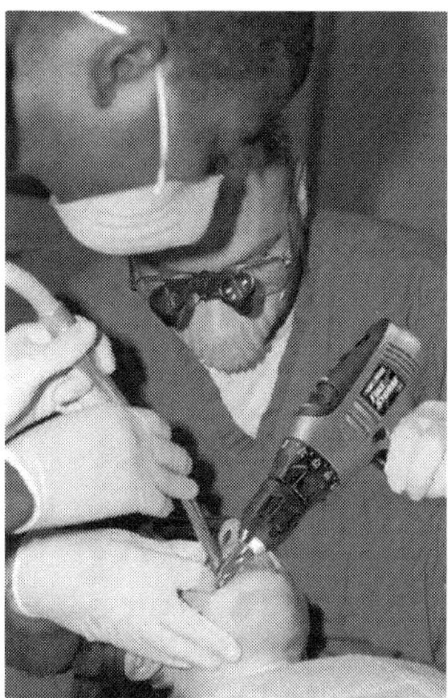

Dental drill for big cavities

Terrible Tommy went to the doctor and the doctor tells him for the test he needed, Tommy would have to save up a urine sample.

That night Tommy went home and asked his mom what a urine sample was. His mom said she didn't know and to ask the lady next door.

Tommy went next door and asked the lady. About ten minutes later he arrived home with scratches all over and had barely any clothes on.

Tommy's mom asked him what happened.

He said, "I did what you said and asked her. She told me to go pee in a cup, so I told her to go crap in a bucket and the fight began."

A Polish immigrant went to the optometrist office for an exam. First, he had to take an eye vision test.

The optician showed him a card with the letters: 'C Z W I X N O S T A C Z'

"Can you read this?" the optician asked.

"Read it?" the Polish guy replied, "I know the guy."

Young lady to father "Daddy, when I grow up shall I become a heart-doctor or a tooth-doctor?"
"I think dentist."
"Why father?"
"We have only one heart, but thirty two teeth."

A patient goes to his doctor, "I can't sleep at night. I keep having the same dream about a door with a sign. I push and push, but I can never get it open."

The doctor asks, "What does the sign say?"
"Pull."

A seventy-five-year-old woman went to the doctor for a check-up. The doctor told her she needed more activity and recommended sex three times a week.

She said to the doctor, "Please, tell my husband."

The doctor went out in the waiting room and told the husband that his wife needed to have sex three times a week.

The eighty year old husband replied, "Which days?"

The doctor said, "How about Monday, Wednesday, and Friday."

The husband answered, "I can bring her Monday and Wednesday, but on Fridays she will have to take the bus."

Did you hear about the X-ray technician who married one of his patients?
Everybody wondered what he saw in her.

The man looked a little worried when the doctor came in to administer his annual physical, so the first thing the doctor did was to ask whether anything was troubling him.

"To tell the truth doc, yes," answered the patient. "You see, I seem to be getting forgetful. I'm never sure I can remember where I put the car, or whether I answered a letter, or where I'm going, or what it is I'm going to do once I get there, if I get there. I really need your help. What can I do?"

The doctor thought about it for a moment, then answered in his kindest tone, "Pay me in advance."

Doctors can be frustrating. You wait a month-and-a-half for an appointment, and they say, "I wish you came to me sooner."

I am so depressed. My doctor refused to write me a prescription for Viagra.

He said it would be like putting a new flagpole on a condemned building.

A man is suffering from extreme headaches so he goes to see his doctor. He arrives and says, “Doctor I have been having these bad headaches and nothing I do seems to cure them.”

The doctor says, “One thing I always do to relieve my headaches is put my head between my wife’s boobs and have her jiggle them until my headache goes away.”

“Thanks doc, I think I’ll try it.”

Two weeks pass and the man goes back to his doctor.

The doctor says, “Have your headaches cleared up?”

“They sure have. I tried what you said. By the way, I love the wall paper in your home.”

Patient: Doctor, I have yellow teeth, what do I do?
Dentist: Wear a brown tie.

One night, as a couple lay down for bed, the husband gently tapped his wife on the shoulder and started rubbing her arm. His wife turned over and said, “I’m sorry honey, I have a gynecologist appointment tomorrow and I want to stay fresh.”

Her husband turned over and tried to sleep. A few minutes later, he rolled back over and tapped his wife again.

This time he whispered in her ear, “Do you have a dentist appointment tomorrow too?”

A woman went to her new doctor for a checkup. He turned out to be absolutely gorgeous. He told her he was going to put his hand on her back and he wanted her to say, ‘Eighty-eight’.

“Eighty-eight,” she purred.

“Good. Now I’m going to put my hand on your throat and I want you to again say, ‘Eighty-eight’.”

“Eighhty. . . eighhhhtttt.”

“Fine. Now I’m going to put my hand on your chest and I want you once more to say, ‘Eighty-eight’.”

“One, two, three, four, five. . .”

An elderly patient went to have her teeth checked. “Mrs. Meiers, your teeth are good for the next fifty years.” the dentist exclaimed.
She replied, “What will they do without me?”

A doctor examined a woman, took the husband aside, and said, “I don’t like the looks of your wife at all.”

“Me neither, doc,” said the husband, “But she’s a great cook and really good with the kids.”

A marine biologist developed a race of genetically engineered dolphins that could live forever if they were fed a steady diet of seagulls. One day, his supply of the birds ran out, so he had to go out and trap some more.

On the way back, he spied two lions asleep on the road. He was afraid to wake them, so he gingerly stepped over them.

He was arrested and charged with *transporting gulls across sedate lions for immortal porpoises.*

The American Medical Association researchers have made a remarkable discovery. It seems that some patients needing blood transfusions may benefit from receiving chicken blood rather than human blood.

It tends to make men cocky and women lay better.

A blonde tried to follow her doctor's advice and give up smoking cigarettes and try chewing gum instead, but the matches kept getting stuck and the gum wouldn't light.

Another blonde went to an eye doctor to have her eyes checked for glasses.

The doctor directed her to read various letters with the left eye while covering the right eye.

The blonde was so mixed up about which eye was which, that the eye doctor, took paper lunch bag with a hole to see through, covered up the appropriate eye and asked her to read the letters.

As he did so, he noticed the blonde had tears streaming down her face.

The doctor comforted her, "There's no need to get emotional about getting glasses."

"I know," agreed the blonde, "But I kind of had my heart set on wire frames."

An elderly gentleman visits his doctor with a complaint of not being able to hear out of his left ear. The exam revealed a rectal suppository in the external auditory canal.

The patient responded, "Now I remember where I misplaced my hearing aid."

What does the dentist of the year get?

A little plaque.

A man went to see his doctor because he was suffering from a miserable cold. His doctor prescribed some pills, but they didn't help.

On his next visit the doctor gave him a shot, and that also did not do any good.

On his third visit the doctor told the man, "Go home, and take a hot bath. As soon as you finish bathing, throw open all the windows and stand in the draft."

"But doc," protested the patient, "If I do that, I'll get pneumonia."

"I know," said the doctor, "I can cure pneumonia."

"Doctor, doctor you have to help me. I keep thinking that I'm a deck of cards."

"Sit over there; I'll deal with you later."

Doctor Jeff had slept with one of his patients and had felt guilty all day long. No matter how much he tried to forget about it, he couldn't. The guilt and sense of betrayal was overwhelming.

However, every once in a while he'd hear that soothing voice, within himself, trying to reassure him. "Jeff, don't worry about it. You aren't the first doctor to sleep with one of their patients and you won't be the last, and you're single. Let it go."

Invariably another voice would bring him back to reality.

"Jeff, you're a vet."

Mother: Has your tooth stopped hurting yet?
Son: I don't know. The dentist kept it

A man takes his son to visit a doctor.
Doctor: What's wrong with him?
Father: He thinks he is a chicken.
Doctor: How long has he been thinking this?
Father: About ten years.
Doctor: Why didn't you bring him to see me before this?
Father: Because we needed the eggs.

Bird Flu

According to archaeologists, for millions of years Neanderthal man was not fully erect.
That's easy to understand considering how ugly Neanderthal women were.

"Open wider." requested the dentist, as he began his examination of the patient. "My goodness!" he said startled. "You've got the biggest cavity I've ever seen - the biggest cavity I've ever seen."

"OK doc," replied the patient. "I'm afraid enough without you saying something like that twice."

"I didn't," said the dentist. "That was the echo."

A man realized he had a lump which was probably a boil, so he went to his doctor. The doctor examined him and determined that it would be necessary to drain the boil.

The doctor offered the man a local anesthetic, but the patient refused it, saying that he'd been hurt two times in his life and after those two painful incidents, he could take any pain.

After he cut and packed the boil, the doctor asked what the two painful incidents had been.

He said, "While on a hunting trip, I needed to defecate, so I went behind a tree, and as I squatted down, the jaws of a bear trap closed on my privates."

"Ouch, and the second painful incident?" asked the doctor.

"When the chain ran out," replied the patient.

Doctor: How is your sister getting along with her reducing diet?
Patient: Just fine, she disappeared last week.

Terrible Tommy was taken to the dentist. It was discovered that he had a cavity that would have to be filled. "Now, young man," asked the dentist, "What kind of filling would you like for that tooth?"

"Chocolate please," replied Tommy.

Why didn't I think of that?

A divorce attorney and a gynecologist were discussing the merits of their professions.

The lawyer said, "I love my work. Every day women come into my office, tell me all their problems, and pay me good money for my advice."

The gynecologist topped him. "In my line of work," he said, "Women come into my office, take off their clothes, tell me their problems, and pay me good money for my advice."

A farmer, who was notoriously miserly, called a doctor to attend his sick wife.
"They say you're a skinflint," said the doctor. "Can I be sure I will receive my fee?"
"Whether you kill my wife or cure her, you will get your money without having to sue," said the farmer.
Unfortunately, the woman died despite all the doctor's efforts to save her. He duly asked for his payment.
"Did you cure my wife?" asked the man.
"No," admitted the doctor.
"Did you kill her?"
"Certainly not," the doctor said indignantly.
"Well then, I owe you nothing."

NEW DOCTOR

A new, young MD doing his residency in OB was quite embarrassed performing female pelvic exams. To cover his embarrassment, he had unconsciously formed a habit of whistling softly.

The middle-aged lady upon whom he was performing this exam suddenly burst out laughing and further embarrassed him.

He looked up from his work sheepishly and said, “I’m sorry. Was I tickling you?”

She replied, “No doctor, but the song you were whistling was ‘I wish I was an Oscar Meyer Wiener’.”

DIAGNOSING

A young doctor had moved out to a small community to replace the retiring country doctor. The older doctor suggested the young one accompany him on his rounds so the community could become familiar with the new doctor.

At the first house a woman complained, “I’ve been a little sick to my stomach.”

The older doctor said, “You have probably been overdoing the fresh fruit. Why not cut back on the amount you have been eating and see if that does the trick?”

As they left the younger man said, “You didn’t even examine that woman. How did you arrive at your diagnosis so quickly?”

“I didn’t have to. You noticed I dropped my stethoscope on the floor in there? When I bent over to pick it up, I noticed a half-dozen banana peels in the trash. That was what was making her sick.”

The younger doctor said, “Very clever. I think I’ll try that at the next house.”

Arriving at the next house, they spent several minutes talking with a younger woman. She complained that she just didn’t have the energy she once did. “I’m feeling terribly run down lately.”

“You have probably been doing too much work for the church,” the young doctor told her. “Perhaps you should cut back a bit and see if that helps.”

As they left, the elder doc said, “Your diagnosis was very interesting. How did you arrive at it?”

“Just as you did at the last house, I dropped my stethoscope and when I bent down to retrieve it, I saw the preacher under the bed.”

ERECTION

A guy goes to a doctor and explains his situation. "Doc, I have a hot date tonight and I want to be sure that I will be able to satisfy her. I need something that will allow me to keep it up all night."

The doctor gives the guy a powerful potion of Cialis and Viagra with other ingredients and warns him to be careful not to take too much.

The guy returns to his apartment and a few minutes before his date was supposed to show for dinner, he slugs down the potion.

The next day he returns to the doctor's office. The guy is in really bad shape. His eyes are sunken, his shirt is tattered, and his penis is swollen, and black and blue.

The guy says to the doctor, "Doc, I need a muscle relaxer."

The doctor looked at the guy's swollen penis and says, "You don't want to put a muscle relaxer on your penis."

"It's not for my penis," he replies. "It's for my arm. My date never showed up last night."

DOCTOR VISIT

I went into my proctologist's office for my first rectal exam. His new nurse Ellie took me to an examining room and told me to get undressed and have a seat until the doctor could see me. She said that he would be in to see me in a few minutes.

After putting on the gown that she gave me I sat down. While waiting, I observed that there were three items on a stand next to the exam table:

A Tube of K-Y jelly, a rubber glove, and a beer.

When the doctor finally came in I said, "Look doc, I'm a little confused.

This is my first exam. I know what the K-Y is for and I know what the glove is for, but can you tell me what the beer is for?"

The doctor became noticeably outraged and stormed over to the door. He flung the door open and yelled to his nurse, "Damn it Ellie, I said a butt light."

SECOND OPINION

A man brought a very limp dog into the veterinary clinic. As he put the dog on the table, the vet pulled out his stethoscope, and placed it on the dog's chest. After a moment, he shook his head sadly and said, "I'm sorry, but your dog has passed away."

"What," screamed the man, "How can you tell? You haven't done any testing on him or even looked close. I want another opinion."

The vet turned and left the room. In a few moments, he returned with a Labrador Retriever. The Retriever went right to work, checking the poor dead dog out thoroughly with his nose. After a considerable amount of sniffing, he too sadly shook his head.

The veterinarian then took the Labrador out and returned in a few minutes with a cat, which also carefully sniffed out the poor dog on the table. As had his predecessors, the cat sadly shook his head. He then jumped off the table and ran out of the room.

The veterinarian handed the man a bill for six hundred dollars.

The dog's owner was wild. "Six hundred dollars just to tell me my dog is dead? This is outrageous."

The vet shook his head and explained, "If you had taken my word for it, the charge would have been fifty dollars, but you also wanted the Lab work and the Cat scan."

VAGINAL EXAM

A middle aged woman was due later in the week for an appointment with the gynecologist. Early one morning she received a call from the doctor's office telling her that she had been rescheduled for early that morning.

She had just packed everyone off to work and school, and it was already around eight-thirty. The trip to his office took about thirty minutes, so she didn't have any time to spare. As most women do, she liked to take a little extra effort over hygiene when making such visits, but this time she wasn't going to be able to make the full effort.

She rushed upstairs, threw off her dressing gown, wet the washcloth that was sitting next to the sink, and gave herself a quick wash in her privates to make sure she was at least presentable. She threw the washcloth in the clothes basket, put on some clothes, hopped in the car, and raced to her appointment.

She was in the waiting room only a few minutes when she was called in. Knowing the procedure, she hopped up on the table, looked over at the other side of the room, and pretended she was in Bermuda or some other place a million miles away.

She was a little surprised when the doctor said, "My, we have made an extra effort this morning, haven't we?" She didn't respond.

When the appointment was over, she heaved a sigh of relief and went home. The rest of the day was uneventful, with shopping, cleaning, cooking, etc.

After school while her young daughter was playing, she called out from the bathroom, "Mom, where's my washcloth?"

The mother told her to get another one from the cupboard. The little girl said she needed the one that was by the sink, "Because it had all my glitter and sparkles in it."

DENTAL PLATE

A Plano man goes to Dr. Marshall Johnson's office, because of a throbbing pain in his mouth.

After a brief examination, Dr. Johnson exclaims, "My goodness, that plate I installed in your mouth about six months ago has nearly completely corroded. What have you been eating?"

"The only thing I can think of is that my wife made me some asparagus about four months ago with some stuff on it called Hollandaise sauce. I have to admit that it was delicious. I have never tasted anything like it. Ever since then, I have been putting it on everything."

"That's probably the reason," replied the dentist, "Hollandaise sauce is made with lemon juice, which is acidic and highly corrosive. It seems as though I will have to install a new plate, but made out of chrome this time."

"Why chrome?" the man asked.

Dr. Johnson replied, "Everyone knows that, *there's no plate like chrome for the Hollandaise.*"

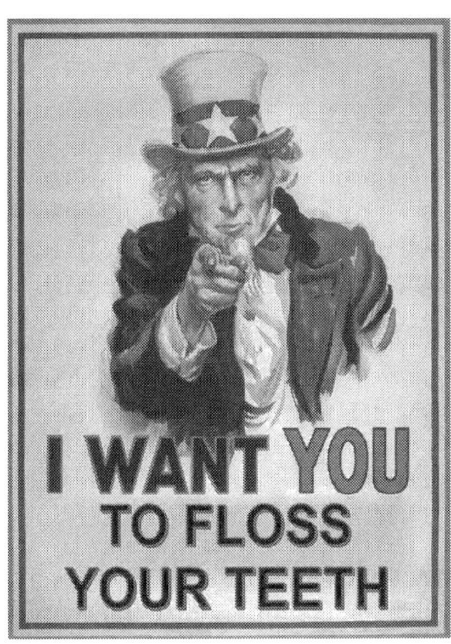

ANNUAL REVIEW

Marc and Kim were in a mental institution. The place had an annual contest and picked two of the best patients to give them two questions. If they answered correctly, they were considered cured and free to go.

Marc was called into the doctor's office first and asked if he understood that he'd be free if he answered the questions correctly. The doctor said, "Marc, what would happen if I poked out one of your eyes?"

Marc said, "I'd be half blind."

"That's correct. What would happen if I poked out both your eyes?"

"I'd be completely blind." The doctor stood up, shook his hand, and told him he was free.

On his way out, Marc mentioned the questions to Kim. He told him what questions would be asked and the correct answers.

Kim was called in.

The doctor went through the formalities and asked, "What would happen if I cut off one of your ears?"

Kim remembered what Marc had said and answered, "I'd be half blind."

The doctor was a bit puzzled, but went on. "What would happen if I cut off both your ears?"

"I'd be completely blind."

"Kim, how can you explain that you would be blind if I cut off your ears?" asked the doctor.

"My hat would fall over my eyes," was Kim's reply.

ADVICE

A woman went to her doctor for advice. She told him that her husband had developed a penchant for anal sex, and she was not sure that it was such a good idea.

The doctor asked, “Do you enjoy it?”

She said that she did.

He asked, “Does it hurt you?”

She said that it did not.

The doctor then told her, “Then, there’s no reason that you shouldn’t practice anal sex, if that’s what you like. Of course you must take precautions so you do not get pregnant.”

The woman was mystified. She asked, “Can a person get pregnant from anal sex?”

The doctor replied, “Of course. Where do you think attorneys come from?”

BROKEN LEG

A man goes to the doctor. He says, “Doc, you have to check my leg. Something is wrong. Put your ear up to my thigh and you will hear it.”

The doctor cautiously placed his ear to the man’s thigh, and heard, “Give me twenty bucks. I really need twenty bucks.”

“I have never seen or heard anything like this before. How long has this been going on?” The doctor asked.

“That’s nothing Doc. Put your ear next to my knee.”

The doctor put his ear to the man’s knee and heard it say, “Man, I really need ten dollars. Come on, lend me a tenner.”

“Sir, I really don’t know what to tell you. I have never witnessed anything like this.”

“Wait doc, that’s not all. There’s more. Put your ear next to my ankle,” the man urged him.

The doctor did as the man said and was amazed to hear his ankle plead, “Please, I just need five dollars. Lend me five. Please.”

“I have no idea what to tell you. The doc said.

He frantically searched all his medical reference books, searched online, and looked at the man. There’s nothing about it in any of my books or the healthcare forums.”

“I do think I can make one well educated guess based on the symptoms,” he continued. “Based on life and all my previous experience, I can tell you that your leg appears to be broke in three places.”

HEARING TEST

An old man decided his old wife was losing her hearing, so he called the doctor to make an appointment to have her hearing checked.

The doctor said he could see her in two weeks, but meanwhile there is a simple and informal test he could do to give the doctor some idea of the dimensions of the problem.

“Here is what you do. Start about forty feet away from her, and speak in a normal conversational tone and see if she hears you. If not, go to thirty feet, twenty feet, and so on until you get a response.”

That evening the wife is in the kitchen cooking dinner, and the husband is in the living room. He thinks to himself, “I’m about forty feet away, let’s see what happens.”

“Honey, what’s for supper?” No response.

He moves to the other end of the room, about thirty feet away.

“Honey, what’s for supper?” No response.

He moves into the dining room, about twenty feet away.

“Honey, what’s for supper?” No response.

He now moves right next to the kitchen door, ten feet away.

“Honey, what’s for supper?”

Still no response, so he walks right up behind her and says, “Honey, what’s for supper?”

She turns and says, “For the fifth time, I said chicken.”

BREAST PROBLEMS

A young Native American woman went to a doctor for her first physical exam. After checking all of her vitals and running the usual tests, the doctor said, “Running Doe, you are in fine health. I could find no problems. I did notice one slight abnormality however.”

“What is that, Doctor?”

“I noticed you have no nipples.”

“None of the people in my tribe have nipples,” she replied.

“That is amazing,” said the doctor. “I’d like to write this up for The Journal of Medicine if you don’t mind.”

Running Doe said, “OK.”

The doctor asked, “How many people are in your tribe?”

She answered, “Approximately five hundred.”

“And what is the name of your tribe?”

Running Doe replied, “We’re called. . . *The Indian nippleless five hundred.*”

UROLOGIST

Phil went to see a Urologist, but before he dropped his pants he asked the doctor not to laugh.

"Of course I won't laugh," the doctor said. "I am a professional. In over twenty years I have never laughed at a patient."

"OK," Phil said, and proceeded to drop his trousers revealing the tiniest thingie the doctor had ever seen. It couldn't have been size of a small peanut.

Unable to control himself, the doctor started giggling, and then fell laughing to the floor. Ten minutes later he was finally able to struggle to his feet and regain his composure.

"I am so sorry," said the doctor. "I really am. I don't know what came over me. On my honor as a professional and a gentleman, I promise it won't happen again. Now what seems to be the problem?"

Phil replied, "It's swollen."

SPERM COUNT

An eighty-year-old man went to his doctor's office to get a sperm count. The doctor gave the man a jar and said, "Take this jar home and bring back a semen sample tomorrow."

The next day the old man reappeared at the doctor's office and gave him the jar, which was as clean and empty as it was on the previous day.

The doctor asked what happened and the man explained, "Well doc, it's like this. First I tried with my right hand, but nothing. Then I tried with my left hand, but still nothing.

Then I asked my wife for help. She tried with her right hand, then her left, still nothing. She tried with her mouth, first with the teeth in, then with her teeth out, and still nothing.

We even called up the lady next door and she tried too, first with both hands, then an armpit and she even tried squeezing it between her knees, but still nothing."

The doctor was shocked and asked, "You asked your neighbor?"

The old man replied, "Yes, and no matter what we tried, we still could not get the darned jar open."

ALTERNATE THERAPY

A doctor has the reputation of helping couples increase the fun in their sex life. He always promises not to take a case if can't help them.

The Browns go to see the doctor. He gives both of them a physical exam, psychological exam, and various other tests.

After checking the results he says, "I am happy to say that I can help you. On your way home stop at the grocery store and buy some grapes and doughnuts. When you get home, take off your clothes, sit on the floor, and you sir, roll the grapes across the floor until you make a bull's-eye in your wife's love tube. Then get on your hands and knees crawl to her like a strong lion and retrieve the grape using only your tongue.

Go back to your original positions, then you madam, must take a doughnut and toss it from across the room at your husband's love pole. When you circle it, crawl like a lioness to him, and consume the doughnut without using your hands."

The couple goes home, try the suggestions, and find their love life has become fantastic.

They tell their friends and suggest that they should see the doctor. The doctor greets the new couple and says he will not take the case if he can not help.

After the usual tests he tells them, "Bad news I can not help you. I believe your sex life is as good as it will ever be."

They plead with him and say, "You helped our friends the Browns so much. Please, please help us."

"OK, I will try one thing," says the doctor.

"On your way home from the office, stop at the grocery store and buy some apples and a box of Cheerios. . ."

IMPOTENCE

After a few years of married life, a man finds he is unable to perform his husbandly duties.

He goes to his doctor, and his doctor tries a few things, but nothing works. Finally the doctor says to him, "This must be all in your mind," and refers him to a psychiatrist.

After a few visits to the shrink, the doc confesses, "I am at a loss as to how you could possibly be cured." After some thought, the psychiatrist refers him to a witch doctor.

The witch doctor says, "I can cure this." He throws powder on a flame and there is a flash with large billowing smoke. The witch doctor says, "This is a powerful healing, but you can only use it once a year. All you have to do is say "123" and it will rise for as long as you wish."

The guy then asks the witch doctor, "What happens when it's over?"

He glances at the man and says "All you or your partner has to say is "1234" and it will go down, but be warned; it will not rise again for a year."

The guy goes home and that night he is ready to surprise his wife with the good news. He is lying in bed with her and says, "123," and suddenly he gets a huge erection.

His wife turns over to him and says, "What did you say, '123' for?"

CASTRATION

Sam, a young man, goes into the doctor's offices and says, "Doc, I want to be castrated."

"Why would you want to do that?" asks the doctor in amazement.

"It's something I've been thinking about for a long time and I want to have it done" replies Sam.

"But have you thought it through properly?" asks the doctor. "It's a very serious operation and once it's done, there's no going back. It will change your life forever."

"I'm aware of that and you are not going to change my mind. Either you book me in to be castrated or I'll go to another doctor."

The doctor replies, "All right, I'll perform the operation. However, it's against my better judgment."

Sam has his operation, and the next day he is up and walking very slowly, legs apart, down the hospital corridor pulling his drip stand along.

Heading towards him is another patient, who is walking exactly the same way.

"Hi there," says Sam. "It looks as if you've just had the same operation as me."

The other patient says, "I finally decided after thirty years of life that I would like to be circumcised."

Sam looks at him in horror and screams, "Damn, that's the word I meant."

THE DENTIST

A man and his wife walk into Dr. Julie Stelly's office to have a tooth pulled.

The man says to the dentist, "Doc, I'm really in a hurry. I have two buddies sitting out in my car waiting for us to go play golf, so forget about the anesthetic and just pull the tooth and be done with it.

We have a ten o'clock tee time at the best golf course in town and it's nine-thirty already. I don't have time to wait for the anesthetic to work."

The dentist thought to herself, "My goodness, this is surely a very brave man, asking to have his tooth pulled without using anything to kill the pain."

So she asks him, "Which tooth is it sir?"

The man turns to his wife and says, "Hurry, open your mouth dear and show him which tooth needs to be pulled."

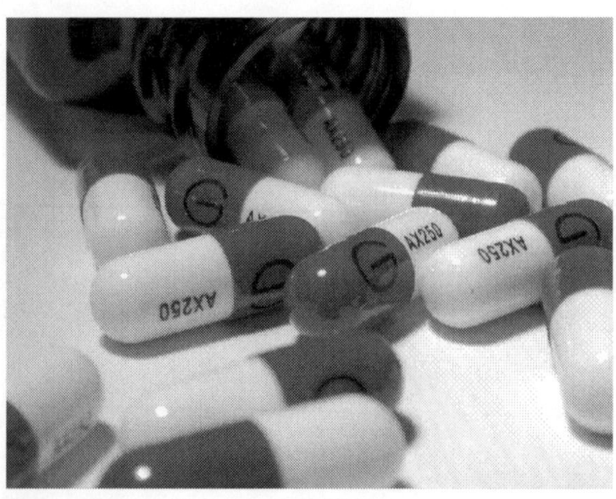

BROKEN SCROTUM

A woman stood up at her church's Testimony Meeting one Sunday morning, took the microphone, and bared her soul to the congregation.

"I want to tell you about the awful accident that my husband Jim has suffered this past month. He was riding his motorcycle, lost control, ran off the highway, and hit a tree. He was rushed to the hospital, and could have died, but thank the Lord, all he suffered was a broken scrotum."

The congregation gasped in horror. The men in the congregation were obviously uneasy and wiggled in their seats.

"Jim has been in terrible pain all month since the accident. He has trouble breathing. He has trouble swallowing his food. He can hardly lift anything, because he is in so much pain. He has even missed work because of it. He can't lift our children up to hold them and give them the personal love that they need. Worst of all, we can no longer cuddle and have intimate relations. He is in constant pain, a pain so terrible that our love life has all but slipped away into oblivion. I would like to ask you all in the congregation to pray for Jim, and pray for us, that his broken scrotum will soon heal and be as good as new."

A dull murmur erupted within the congregation as the full impact of this terrible accident sunk in, and the men in the congregation were visibly shaken up with the ugly possibilities.

As the murmuring settled down, a lone figure stood up in midst of the congregation, worked his way up to the pulpit, obviously in pain, adjusted the microphone, leaned over, and said to the congregation,

"My name is Jim, and I have only one word for my wife. That word is sternum. I told you, sternum."

PAIN KILLER

A man walks into the dentist's office and after the dentist examines him, he says, "That tooth has to come out. I'm going to give you a shot of Novocain and I'll be back in a few minutes."

The man grabs the dentist's arm, "No way. I hate needles I'm not having any shot."

So the dentist says, "OK, we'll have to go with gas."

"Absolutely not," the man replies. It makes me very sick for a couple of days. I'm not having gas."

The dentist steps out and comes back with a glass of water, "Here," he says, "Take this pill."

The man asks, "What is it?"

"Viagra," answers the dentist.

The man looks surprised and asks, "Will that kill the pain?"

"No, but it will give you something to hang on to while I pull your tooth."

RASH

A young lady went to the doctor for a checkup. The doctor started looking her over and noticed a rash, in the shape of a “Y,” on her chest.

When he asked her to explain its origin, she stammered, “Uh, my boyfriend goes to Yale, and, well, he likes to make love with his sweater on.”

“That’s no problem,” said the doctor, and he gave her a tube of RashAway.

A few days later, a second young lady went to see the same doctor. When the doctor began examining the second young lady, he noticed she had an “H” shaped rash on her chest.

When he asked her to explain its origin, she stammered, “Well, my boy friend goes to Harvard, and he likes to make love with his sweater on.”

“That is not a problem,” said the doctor, and he gave her a tube of RashAway.

A few weeks later, a third young lady went to the same doctor. When the doctor started checking her over, he noticed she had an “M” shaped rash on her chest.

“Don’t tell me,” said the doctor, “Your boyfriend goes to Michigan and he likes to make love with his sweater on?”

“It’s not exactly like that,” said the woman, “My girlfriend goes to Wisconsin and. . .”

PREMATURE

A man was having problems with premature ejaculation, so he decided to go to the doctor.

When he arrived, he asked the doctor what he could do to cure his problem. In response, the doctor said, "When you feel like you are getting ready to ejaculate, try startling yourself."

That same day, the man went to the store and bought himself a starter pistol. He was all excited to try this suggestion and he ran home to his wife. He arrived home and found his wife was in bed, naked and waiting.

As the two began, they found themselves in the sixty-nine position. Moments later, the man felt the sudden urge to ejaculate and fired the starter pistol.

The next day, the man went back to the doctor.

The doctor asked, "How did it go?"

The man answered, "Not that well. When I fired the pistol, my wife peed on my face, bit three inches off my penis, and my neighbor came out of the closet with his hands in the air."

PHYSICIAN TYPES

Dentists: Not very nice people - they get on your nerves. They are always down in the mouth.

Dermatologist: This doctor builds his business from scratch. He has two mottoes on his shingle, which is on his left arm.

Obstetrician: Works in the 'ladies-ready-to-bear' department at the local general hospital.

Opthalmologist: A wonderful persons - a sight for sore eyes. Drinks too much and often makes a spectacle of himself.

Osteopath: Very proud of the profession and make no bones about it. Very generous, always twisting your arm or pulling your leg.

Podiatrist: As a student, always aspired to get to the foot of the class. Podiatrists are not to be trusted - they are generally heels, and your arch enemy.

Psychiatrist: A mind sweeper. A freudy cat.

Radiologist: Very, very friendly, love everyone. Sometimes difficult to understand what they see in people.

Tree Surgeon: A dangerous profession. Many tree surgeons have been known to fall out of their patients. Generally appear to be surly characters, but their bark is worse than their bite. Usually work out of a branch office.

CHINESE MEDICINE

A gentleman permitted himself one minor indiscretion and found that after a few days he had contracted a devastating social disease. He immediately went to the doctor.

The doctor advised him to have his pecker amputated to avoid the risk of spreading to other vital organs. The cost would be about two thousand dollars.

This terribly upset the man who felt there must be a better way to take care of his problem.

He went to another physician for a second opinion and was again told that it must be cut off for his health's sake. The cost would be about four thousand dollars.

After discussing the matter with an associate, he discovered that there was a Chinese doctor that might be able to help and that his charges would certainly be lower than the western surgeons.

He went to see the Chinese physician and had a complete and thorough checkup.

The physician told him, "These American doctors are just out to take your money. If you just wait for a few weeks, it will fall off by itself."

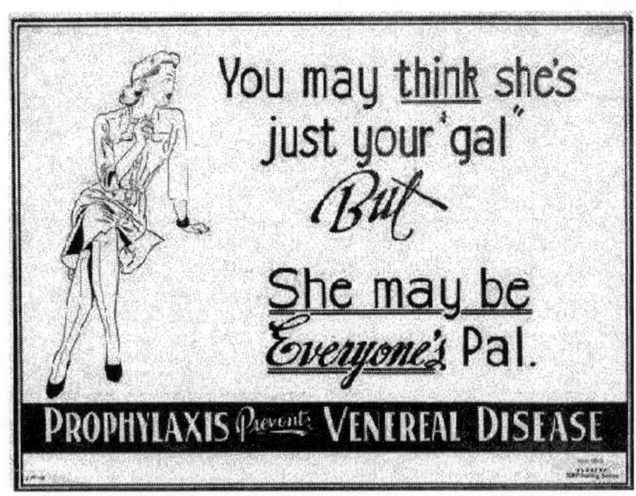

TESTICLE PROBLEMS

A midget from Dallas, Texas went to Doctor Louis Torres because his testicles ached almost all the time.

The doctor told him to stand on the examining table and drop his pants. The doc put one finger under his left testicle and told the midget to turn his head and cough.

"Aha!" he mumbled and putting his finger under the right testicle, he asked the midget to turn and cough again.

"Aha!" said Dr. Torres again and reached for his surgical scissors. Snip, snip on the right side and snip, snip on the left side.

The midget was so scared that he was afraid to look, but noticed with amazement that the snipping did not hurt.

The doctor then told the midget to get dressed and see if his testicles still ached.

The midget was absolutely delighted as he walked around the office and discovered his testicles were no longer aching.

The midget said, "Perfect doc, and I didn't even feel it. What type of operation did you do?"

The doctor replied, "I cut two inches of leather off the top of each of your cowboy boots."

DOCTOR ACE

A rather flat-chested young lady went to Doctor Ace for advice about enlarging her breasts.

He explained his technique her, “Everyday when you get out of the shower, rub your nipples and say, “Scooby doobie doobies, I want bigger boobies.”

She did this faithfully for several months, and it worked. She grew very large boobs.

One morning she was running late and when she was on the bus she realized she had forgotten her morning ritual. At this point she loved her new boobs and didn’t want to lose them, so she got up, right in the middle of the bus, and said, ”Scooby doobie doobies, I want bigger boobies.”

A guy was sitting nearby and asked her, “Do you go to Doctor Ace by any chance?”

“Why yes, I do. How did you know?”

He leaned toward her and whispered, “Hickory dickory dock.”

EXAMINATION

A woman went to her local clinic. She was seen by one of the new doctors and after about five minutes in the examination room, she burst out screaming as she ran down the hall.

An older doctor stopped and asked her what the problem was, and she explained the situation to him.

The doctor had her sit down and relax in another room.

The older doctor marched back to the new young doctor and demanded, “What’s the matter with you?

Mrs. Luna is sixty-five years old. She has two grown children and four grandchildren. How could you tell her she was pregnant?”

The new doctor continued writing on his clipboard and asked, “Does she still have the hiccups?”

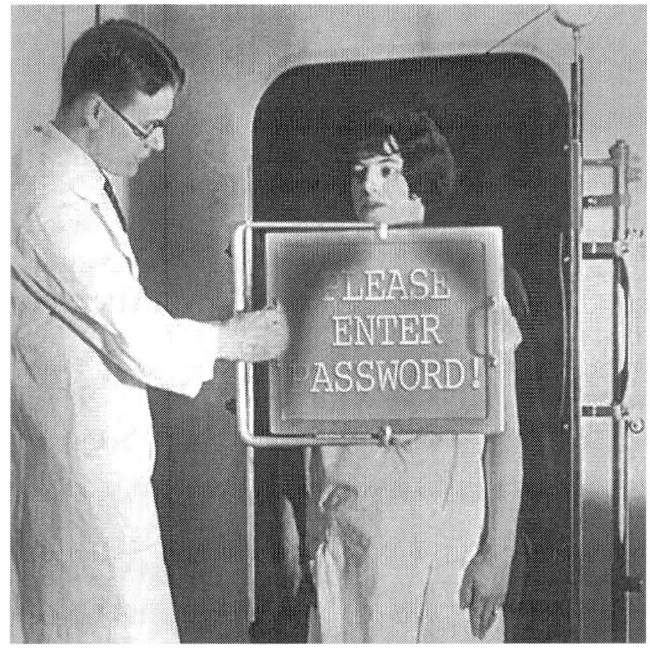

GYNECOLOGIST VISIT

A beautiful, voluptuous woman went to a gynecologist. The doctor took one look at this woman and all his professionalism went out the window. He immediately told her to undress.

After she disrobed the doctor began to stroke her thigh. As he did this, he asked her, “Do you know what I’m doing?”

“Yes,” she replied, “You’re checking for any abrasions or dermatological abnormalities.”

“That is right,” said the doctor.

He then began to fondle her breasts. “Do you know what I’m doing now?”

“Yes,” the woman said, “You’re checking for any lumps or breast cancer.”

“Correct,” replied the shifty doctor.

Finally, he mounted his patient and started having sexual intercourse with her. He asked, “Do you know what I’m doing now?”

“Yes,” she said.

“You’re getting herpes, which is why I came in here to see you in the first place.”

CRUTCHES

One day, Mike Walling noticed that his penis was growing larger and staying erect longer.

Needless to say, he was delighted, and so was his wife.

After several weeks, and nearly nine inches of additional length, Mike became concerned and the couple went to see a Urologist.

After an initial examination, the physician explained to the couple that the man's condition was very rare, but could be cured through corrective surgery.

"How long will he be on crutches?" Mike's wife asked anxiously.

"Crutches?" responded the surprised doctor.

"Yes," she replied, "You are planning to lengthen his legs, aren't you?

RARE CONDITION

Jeff Flanagan was moderately successful in his career with ING, but as he aged he was increasingly hampered by incredible headaches. When his personal hygiene and love life began to suffer, he sought medical help. After being referred from one specialist to another, he finally came across a doctor who could solve the problem.

"The good news is I can cure your headaches. The bad news is that it will require castration. You have a very rare condition which causes your testicles to press up against the base of your spine. The pressure creates one heck of a headache. The only way to relieve the pressure is to remove the testicles."

Jeff was shocked and depressed. He wondered if he had anything to live for. He couldn't concentrate long enough to answer, but decided he had no choice but to go under the knife.

When he left the hospital his mind was clear, but he felt like he was missing an important part of himself. As he walked down the street, he realized that he felt like a different person. He could make a new beginning and live a new life.

Flanagan walked past a men's clothing store and thought, "That's what I need, a new suit." He entered the shop and told the salesman Brad, "I'd like a new suit."

Brad eyed him briefly and said, "Let's see. . . size 46 long."

Jeff laughed, "That's right, how did you know?"

"It's my job."

Jeff tried on the suit. It fit perfectly. As he admired himself in the mirror, the salesman asked, "How about a new shirt?" Jeff thought for a moment and said, "Sure."

Brad eyed him and said, "Let's see, sleeve 35 and 17 1/2 neck." Jeff was surprised, "That's right, how did you know?"

"It's my job."

Jeff tried on the shirt, and it fit perfectly. As he adjusted the collar in the mirror, the salesman asked, "How about new shoes?"

Jeff was on a roll and said, "Good idea."

The salesman eyed Joe's feet and said, "Let's see, 11 medium." Jeff was astonished, "That's right, how did you know?"

"It's my job."

Flanagan was feeling great, when Brad asked, "How about some new underwear?"

He thought for a second, and said, "Sure, why not."

The salesman stepped back, eyed Jeff's waist and said, "Let's see. . . size 38."

Jeff laughed, "No, I've worn size 36 since I was 18 years old."

Brad shook his head, "You can't wear a size 36. It would press your testicles up against the base of your spine and give you one heck of a headache."

LENBUSH CURE

The new doctor that came to town could cure anything and anybody.

Everyone was impressed, except Smith, the town grouch. Smith swore he would prove this new doctor wasn't anything special.

He told the doctor that he had lost his sense of taste. "I can't taste anything, doc. What can you do for me?"

The doctor thought a moment and told Smith, "All you need is the Lenbush Cure."

"Lenbush Cure?" Smith asked.

The doctor presented a jar and told Smith to taste it.

He did and immediately spat it out. "That's gross," he yelled.

"Correct, Mister Smith," said the doctor. "I just restored your sense of taste."

Smith went home mad, plotting his revenge. A month later, he was sure he had a problem the new guy could not cure.

"Doc, I can't remember anything."

The doctor thought a moment and then said, "What you need is the Lenbush Cure."

Before the doctor could get the jar, Smith ran from the office.

WRONG DOCTOR

Signs You Have the Wrong Doctor

Directions to his office include the phrase, “Turn off the paved road.”

Magazines in the waiting room include, ‘Juggs’, ‘Cracked’, and ‘Mad’.

Medical diploma on the wall appears to be the warranty from a craftsman cordless screwdriver.

Question number six on the patient questionnaire is, “Are you the type who is likely to press charges?”

He is wearing the pair of pants you gave to goodwill last month.

All the tongue depressors have a faint taste of fudgesicle.

You don’t seem to remember Viagra coming in different colors with little m’s on them.

Your stress test consists of an appearance with your relatives on ‘The Jerry Springer show’.

He giggles uncontrollably whenever he hears the word rectum.

His answer to dubious test results is, “Oh well, let’s all do a shot.

Bacon cures anything

STUDENT PROCTOLOGIST

A student of proctology was in the morgue one day after classes, wanting to get some practice in before the final exams.

He went over to a table where a corpse was lying face down and uncovered the body. He looked down and found a cork in the corpse's rectum.

He thought this was fairly unusual, so he pulled the cork out and was stunned when music began playing, "On the road again, just can't wait to get on the road again."

The student was amazed and popped the cork back into the anus. As he did so, the music stopped.

The student called the Medical Examiner over and said, "Look at this. It's amazing." The student again pulled the cork out.

They both heard, "On the road again, just can't wait to get on the road again."

"So what?" the Medical Examiner replied.

"But isn't that the most amazing thing you have ever seen?" asked the student.

"Are you kidding?" answered the examiner. "Any butthole can sing country music."

OUTPATIENTS

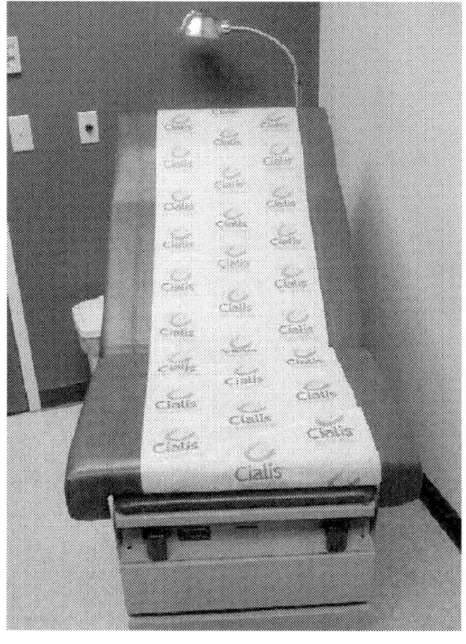

ODDS AND ENDS

If you think health care is expensive now, wait until you see what it costs when it's free.

A man called his doctor and told him he had a problem with his wife, because she has a bowel movement at seven o'clock every morning.
"That's perfectly normal," the doctor said.
"But we don't get out of bed until nine."

A doctor and his wife were having a big argument at breakfast. "You aren't good in bed, either." he shouted and stormed off to work. By midmorning, he decided he better make amends and phoned home. After many rings, his wife picked up the phone.
"What took you so long to answer?"
"I was in bed."
"What are you doing in bed this late?"
"Getting a second opinion."

"I've had a terrible time. I was so ill, I didn't even want to talk about it !"

At a Health Clinic, an older woman found one reason or another to visit daily. She had few friends and liked to chat with the doctors and nurses.

They in turn treated all of her medical complaints with seeming concern and compassion.

Showing up one afternoon, after being absent for over a week, a nurse asked her why she hadn't been there in so long.

The lady responded, "I've been sick all week."

A biology major was taking a cell biology course. The task of the day was examining epithelial cheek cells under a microscope. They had to scrape the inside of their mouths with a toothpick, make a slide from it, and record the different types of cells that were found.

One girl in the class was having a difficult time trouble identifying some cells. She called the professor over to ask him. After a moment or two of peering in her scope, he looked up and said, "Those are sperm cells."

Mid-life is when you are so old that you realize you have to pay someone to see you naked.

Heart Attacks - God's revenge for eating His animal friends.

"I'm having trouble with this new hearing aid," said the man to his audiologist.

"Really? Can you describe the symptoms?"

"Sure. Homer is fat and yellow, Marge has blue hair. . ."

What's the difference between a bartender and a proctologist?
A proctologist takes care of only one asshole at a time.

The teacher announced a spelling test and asked each child in the class to tell what his or her father did for a living and spell the occupation.

Chucky went first, "My dad's a baker, and if he were here he would give you a hot cross bun. 'b-a-k-e-r'."

Susie was next, "My dad's a gynecologist, and if he were here he'd give. . ."

"That's fine," teacher interrupted nervously. "Tommy, it's your turn."

Tommy stood up, "My dad's a bookie, b-o-o-k-i-e, and if he were here he'd give you ten-to-one that Susie's never gonna spell gynecologist."

The optometrist fell into a lens grinder. He made an awful spectacle of himself.

"We all know you can get AIDS from sex,
but we also know at least one President got sex from aides?"

A blonde walks into work, and both of her ears are all bandaged up.
The boss asks, "What happened to your ears?"
She says, "Yesterday I was ironing a skirt when the phone rang and SSSSS. . . I accidentally answered the iron."
The boss says, "That explains one ear, but what about your other ear?"
She says, "I had to call the doctor."

To lengthen thy life, lessen thy meals.

Most doctors do it with patience, some doctors do it with patients.

Mike just turned eighty and went to the doctor to get a physical.

A few days later the doctor saw Mike walking down the street with a gorgeous young woman on his arm. The doctor walked up to him and said, "You're really doing great, aren't you?"

Mike replied, "Just doing what you said, doc. Get a hot mama and be cheerful."

The doctor replied, "That's not exactly what I said. I said, 'You've got a heart murmur. Be careful'."

He was so cheap that he died of oneberculosis.

I once knew a physician who loved frozen daiquiris. He was at a bar one night drinking one when a piece of hickory-wood from the ceiling fell into the glass. The bartender said, "It's a hickory daiquiri, doc."

Doctor, doctor, I think I'm shrinking.
Well you'll just have to be a little patient.

A man goes to a psychiatrist and says, "Doctor, my wife is unfaithful to me. Every evening, she goes to Larry's bar and picks up men. In fact, she goes to bed with anybody who asks her. I'm going crazy. What do you think I should do?"

"Relax," says the doctor, "Take a deep breath and calm down. Now, tell me, where exactly is Larry's bar?"

“Today,” said the professor, “I will be lecturing about the liver and spleen.”

One med student leaned toward the other, “Darn, if there’s one thing I can’t stand it’s an organ recital.”

Why do women like to go to old gynecologists?
Because they shake.

Did you hear about the Irish abortion clinic? There’s a twelve-month waiting list.

Charley Horse - A muscle cramp This originated in the 1600s, when Charles I of England expanded the London police force and the new recruits were nicknamed ‘Charleys’.

There wasn’t enough money to provide the new police with horses so they patrolled on foot and joked that their sore feet came from riding ‘Charley’s horse’.

🕑 ⌛ 🕓

What has thick glasses and a wet nose?
A nearsighted gynecologist.

🕑 ⌛ 🕓

In the middle of an international gynecology conference, American and French gynecologists are discussing various cases they've recently treated.

French Gynecologist: Only last week, zer was a woman ooh came to see me, and er cleetoris - eet was like a melon.

American Gynecologist: Don't be absurd, it couldn't have been that big. My goodness, she wouldn't have been able to walk.

French Gynecologist: Aaah, you Americans, zare you go again, always talkeeng about ze size. I was talkeeng about ze flavor.

🕑 ⌛ 🕓

Did you hear about the miracle of AIDS?
It turns fruits into vegetables.

🕑 ⌛ 🕓

Does it bother you that doctors call what they do practice?

🕑 ⌛ 🕓

Congress wants medicine to raise the bar and
Medicine wants congress to stop barring raises.

🕑 ⌛ 🕓

A doctor has some trouble with the sink, on a public holiday. He calls the local plumber, only to be told it's his day off. "But I get called out on my days off, too," says the exasperated doctor.

The plumber relents and arrives, glances over the sink, looking preoccupied. He mumbles something about golf, then hands the doctor a couple of aspirin and walks out, saying, "Put these in. If it doesn't clear up in twenty four hours, call me back."

🕑 ⌛ 🕘

An Englishman wanted to become an Irishman, so he visited a doctor to find out how to go about this.

The doctor said, "This is a very delicate operation and there is a lot that can go wrong. I will have to remove half your brain."

"That's OK," said the Englishman. "I have always wanted to be Irish and I am prepared to take the risk."

The operation went ahead, but the Englishman woke to find a look of horror on the face of the doctor.

"I am so terribly sorry," the doctor said. "Instead of removing half the brain, I have taken the whole brain out."

The patient replied, "No worries, mate."

🕑 ⌛ 🕘

Tommy was examining his testicles while taking a bath. "Mom," he asks, "Are these my brains?"

"Not yet," replies his mother.

🕑 ⌛ 🕘

Notice all those people who walk around with water bottles, sucking on them as if they were virtual nipples?

In a number of carefully controlled trials, scientists have demonstrated that if we drink one liter of water each day, at the end of the year we would have absorbed more than one kilo of Escherichia Coli. The E. Coli bacteria that is found in feces. In other words, we are consuming one whole kilo of poop.

However, we do not run that risk when drinking wine and beer (or tequila, rum, whiskey, etc.,) because alcohol has to go through a purification process of boiling, filtering, and fermenting. Remember that water equals poop. Booze equals health.

This proves that it is better to drink booze and talk stupid, than to drink water and be full of shit.

🕑 ⌛ 🕘

Number one work related injury

🕑 ⌛ 🕘

Did you hear about the guy whose whole left side was cut off? He's all right now.

🕑 ⌛ 🕘

One morning a woman was over visiting a doctor's house when her daughter-in-law called, in a panic. It seems that her son had just swallowed a penny.

The daughter-in-law wanted her to ask the doctor if she should bring the boy in to be seen.

The doctor calmly replied, "I don't think it's necessary. Just watch him closely for any change."

🕑 ⌛ 🕘

A British technology company has developed a computer chip that will allow women to store music in their breasts.

Seems like this is a major breakthrough, since women often complain about men who stare at their breasts, but don't listen to them.

Terrible Tommy had an earache and wanted a pain killer. He tried in vain to take the lid off the bottle. His mom explained it was a child-proof cap and she would have to open it for him. Tommy asked, "How does it know it's me?"

"Penis Enlargement Clinic"

An Indian chief was feeling very sick, so he summoned the medicine man. After a brief examination, the medicine man took out a long, thin strip of elk rawhide and gave it to the chief, telling him to bite off, chew, and swallow one inch of the leather every day. After a month, the medicine man returned to see how the chief was feeling. The chief shrugged and said, "The thong is ended, but the malady lingers on."

What's the difference between an oral thermometer and a rectal thermometer?

The taste.

🕑 ⌛ 🕘

Three students were sitting around talking between classes, one of the students insisted that the human body must have been designed by an electrical engineer because of the perfection of the nerves and synapses.

Another disagreed, and exclaimed that it had to have been a mechanical engineer who designed the human body. The system of levers and pulleys is ingenious.

"No," the third student said. "You are both wrong. The human body was designed by an architect. Who else but an architect would have put a toxic waste line through a recreation area?"

🕑 ⌛ 🕘

A doctor and a lawyer were talking at a party. Their conversation was constantly interrupted by people describing their ailments and asking the doctor for free medical advice. After an hour of this, the exasperated doctor asked the lawyer, "What do you do to stop people from asking you for legal advice when you're out of the office?"

"I give it to them," replied the lawyer. "Then I send them a bill."

The doctor was shocked, but agreed to give it a try. The next day, he was still feeling a bit guilty, but he prepared the bills. When he went to place them in his mailbox, he found a bill from the lawyer.

🕑 ⌛ 🕘

The doctor asked Terrible Tommy, "How can you prevent diseases caused by biting insects?"
Tommy replied, "Don't bite any."

🕑 ⌛ 🕘

Phil calls his boss one morning and tells him that he is staying home because he is not feeling well.
"What's the matter?" he asks.
"I have a case of anal glaucoma," he says in a weak voice.
"What the heck is anal glaucoma?"
"I can't see my butt coming into work today."

🕑 ⌛ 🕒

An unprepared student sat in his Anatomy class, staring at a question on the final exam paper. The question directed, "Give four advantages of breast milk." "What to write?" he sighed, and began to scribble whatever came into his head, hoping for the best.

1. No need to boil.

2. Never goes sour.

3. Available whenever necessary.

So far so good, but the exam demanded a fourth answer. Once more, he sighed. He frowned. He scowled, and then sighed again. Suddenly, his face brightened, grabbed his pen, and he scribbled his answer.

4. Available in attractive containers of varying sizes.

He received an A.

🕑 ⌛ 🕒

🕑 ⌛ 🕒

Your heart rate can rise as much as 30% during a yawn.

🕑 ⌛ 🕘

A coed went to her doctor for a checkup for the cheerleader squad medical waiver form. Late that afternoon, she returned, looking perplexed but happy.

"How did it go?" asked her roommate.

"I can't go out for the squad, but the doctor really likes me."

"How do you know that?" asked her roommate.

"After he gave me the full physical, he said that I had acute angina."

🕑 ⌛ 🕘

A pipe burst in a doctor's house, so he called a plumber. The plumber arrived, unpacked his tools, did mysterious plumber-type things for a while, and handed the doctor a bill for six hundred dollars.

The doctor exclaimed, "This is ridiculous. I don't even make that much as a doctor."

The plumber waited for him to finish and quietly said, "Neither did I when I was a doctor."

🕑 ⌛ 🕘

Your body is creating and killing fifteen million red blood cells per second.

🕑 ⌛ 🕘

A redhead, brunette, and a blonde went to see their obstetrician. The redhead was trying to make conversation and said, "I'm going to have a boy. I'm sure of it, because I was on top."

The brunette said, "I'm going to have a girl, because I was on the bottom."

The blonde woman suddenly burst into tears. The other women tried to comfort her and asked what was wrong.

"I think I'm going to have puppies," she sobbed.

Your brain is eighty percent water.

A man gets a telephone call from a doctor. The doctor says, “About this medical test I did on you, I have some good news and some bad news.” The man asks for the good news first.

“The good news is you have twenty four hours to live.”

The patient asks, “If that is the good news, then what is the bad news?”

“I couldn’t reach you on the phone yesterday.”

Your heart beats over 100,000 times a day.

One day, a painter found himself short of help and went to the unemployment office to hire someone for the day. When he arrived, they didn’t have any painters available, but they did have a gynecologist there. He reluctantly took the doctor along to help.

A couple of weeks later, the painter returned to the office needing temporary help again. This time there were two painters, but instead he asked for the gynecologist again.

The clerk asked, “Why do you want a gynecologist when we have two professional painters you can take right now?”

He said, “Two weeks ago when I hired the gynecologist, we arrived at the house and it was locked with nobody home. That gynecologist stuck his hand through the mail slot and painted the whole house.”

AILMENTS

Bill Bell is having difficulty to he went to his doctor, walked into a crowded waiting room, and approached the desk.

The receptionist said, "Yes sir, what are you seeing the doctor for today?"

"There's something wrong with my pecker," Bill replied.

The receptionist was irritated and said, "You shouldn't come into a crowded waiting room and say things like that."

"Why not? You asked me what was wrong and I told you," he said.

The receptionist replied, "Now you've caused some embarrassment in this room full of people. You should have said there is something wrong with your ear or something else, and then discussed the problem further with the doctor in private."

Bill replied, "You shouldn't ask people questions in a room full strangers if the answer could embarrass anyone."

He walked out, waited several minutes, and then re-entered.

The receptionist smiled smugly and asked, "May I help you?"

"There's something wrong with my ear," he stated.

The receptionist smiled, knowing he had taken her advice. "And what is wrong with your ear, sir?"

"I can't piss out of it," Bill replied.

BIRTH CONTROL

After having their tenth child, an Alabama couple decided that was enough.

The husband went to his doctor and told him that he and his wife didn't want to have any more children.

The doctor said there was a procedure called a vasectomy that could fix the problem.

The doctor told the man that he was to go home, get a cherry bomb, light it, put it in a can, then hold the can up to his ear and count to ten.

The man said to the doctor, "I may not be the smartest man, but I don't see how putting a lighted cherry bomb in a can and holding it next to my ear is going to help me."

So the couple drove to Missouri to get a second opinion.

The doctor was just about to tell them about the procedure for a vasectomy when he noticed they were from Alabama. This doctor also told the man to go home and get a cherry bomb, light it and place it in a tin can, hold it next to his ear and count to ten.

Figuring that both doctors couldn't be wrong, the man went home, lit a cherry bomb, and put it in a can. He held the can up to his ear and began to count, 1, 2, 3, 4, 5. . . at this point, he paused, placed the can between his legs, and resumed counting on his other hand.

HOUSE CALL

In the back woods of Arkansas, Mister Redd's wife went into labor in the middle of the night and the doctor was called out to assist in the delivery.

To keep the nervous father-to-be busy, the doctor handed him a lantern and said, "Here, you hold this high so I can see what I'm doing."

Soon, a little baby boy was brought into the world.

"Whoa there Lewis," said the doctor. "Don't be in a rush to put the lantern down. I think there's yet another one to come."

Sure enough, within minutes he had delivered another little baby.

"No, no, don't be in a great hurry to put down that lantern, young man. It seems there is yet another one."

The new father scratched his head in bewilderment, and asked the doctor, "Do ye think it's the light that's attracting them?"

Where babies are born?

REFERRAL NOTES

Dermatology OPD Summary

We investigated this patient for latex sensitivity. She gets pinking of her lips when she blows up balloons. She has also had problems with intercourse that may have been related to condom exposure. I could see no point in re-prick testing her.

Medical Outpatient Clinic Summary

Fundoscopy revealed second-degree hemorrhoids, but nothing more sinister.

Referral to Orthopedist

I should be grateful if you could see Mrs. Y, who has halitosis of both great toes.

Referral to a Pediatrician

Kindly see four-year-old James, who has had a cough since yesterday. Also, the family pet dog has had a similar barking cough for the last few days.

Gynecologist's letter to a GP

Thank you for referring this patient. Her leaking occurs with coughing, sneezing, and exercise, such as running. She would like to do more exercise, but the incontinence inhibits her. She does however, carry on swimming.

Urology Clinic Summary

I saw Mr. X in my surgery on January 17. He complained of impudence during sexual intercourse and I wonder if this is related to his beta-blocker.

Medical Outpatient Summary

This lady's blood pressure was 110/65 today. She has a long history of sensual hypertension.

Referral to a Physician

Thanks for seeing this delightful young man with a BP of 170/100. I think we ought to exclude another cause apart from sensual.

Referral to Urologist

I would be grateful if you would see this man, who is complaining of impertinence.

Letter to a lady expecting her first child

Dear Lucy, We have been informed that you are pregnant by your GP. Your local team of midwives will be contacting you shortly.

Surgical Discharge Summary

I think this patient's RIF pain may be due to something like a crumbling appendix.

ADDICTION THERAPY

A man went to his doctor, seeking help for his terrible addiction to cigars.

The doctor was quite familiar with his very compulsive patient, so he recommended an unusual and quite drastic form of aversion therapy.

"When you go to bed tonight, take one of your cigars, unwrap it, and stick it completely up your butt. Then remove it, rewrap it, and place it back with all the others. Do this in such a fashion so you can't tell which one it is. The aversion is obvious. You won't dare smoke any of them, not knowing which is the treated cigar."

"Thanks doc, I'll try it."

Three weeks later he came back and saw the doctor again and reported that the therapy did not work.

"My recommendation didn't work? It was supposed to be effective even in the most addictive of cases, such as yours is," answered the doctor.

"Well, it kind of worked, doc. At least I was able to transfer my addiction," replied the patient.

"What did you transfer your addiction to?" asked the doctor.

"I don't smoke cigars anymore, but now I can't go to sleep at night unless I have a cigar shoved up my butt."

OB GYN

A retired OB GYN doctor decides he is bored and wants to find something to do with his spare time. He always had a motorcycle and loves riding them, but never had enough time to work on them.

Now he decided to go to school to learn to be a master motorcycle mechanic.

After a couple of years of hard studying and learning about bikes, the last day of school was a final exam. The final exam was a two part test.

Part one was diagnostics of a badly running motorcycle engine. Part two everyone in the class had to completely tear down the bike's engine, repair it and put it back together running perfect.

After several hours of working, the teacher tells everyone to stop what they are doing. He then judges everyone's work.

He grades everyone. He tells everyone their scores. The grades are in two parts, fifty points for diagnosis and fifty points for installation.

He gives the first person eighty, another person seventy five, another sixty five.

Finally he gets to the doc's bike, cranks it up, it runs perfect. He gives the doc a hundred and fifty.

He is surprised and asks the teacher why he gave him a hundred and fifty.

The teacher explains to him, "Fifty points for proper diagnosis, fifty points for repairing it properly."

The doc asks what about the other fifty points.

The teacher replies, "In all my life, I've never, seen anyone completely tear down and rebuild a motorcycle engine through the exhaust pipe."

WISE VET

The only cow in a small town in Texas stopped giving milk. The people did some research and found they could buy a cow up in Wisconsin, for five hundred dollars.

They bought the cow from Wisconsin and the cow was wonderful. It produced a great quantity of milk all of the time, and the people were pleased.

They decided to acquire a bull to mate with the cow and produce more cows like it, so they would never have to worry about their milk supply again.

They bought a bull and put it in the pasture with their beloved cow. However, whenever the bull came close to the cow, the cow would move away.

No matter what approach the bull tried, the cow would move away from the bull and he could not succeed in his quest.

The people were very upset and decided to ask the wise veterinarian what to do.

They told the vet what was happening. “Whenever the bull approaches our cow, she moves away. If he approaches from the back, she moves forward. When he approaches her from the front, she backs off. An approach from the side and she walks away to the other side.”

The vet thought about it for a minute and asked, “Did you buy this cow in Wisconsin?”

The people were amazed since they had never mentioned where they bought the cow. “You are truly a wise person,” they said. “How did you know the cow came from Wisconsin?”

The vet replied, “My wife is from Wisconsin.”

TIME

Bob Bonomi is strolling past the mental hospital and suddenly remembers an important meeting.

Unfortunately, his watch has stopped, and he cannot tell if he is late or not. Then, he notices a patient similarly strolling about within the hospital fence.

Calling out to the patient, Bob says, "Pardon me, sir, but do you have the time?"

The patient calls back, "One moment!" and throws himself upon the ground, pulling out a short stick as he does. He pushes the stick into the ground, and, pulling out a carpenter's level, assures himself that the stick is vertical.

With a compass, the patient locates north and with a steel ruler, measures the precise length of the shadow cast by the stick.

Withdrawing a slide rule from his pocket, the patient calculates rapidly, then swiftly packs up all his tools and turns back to the pedestrian, saying, "It is now precisely 3:29 pm, provided today is August 16th, which I believe it is."

Bonomi can't help but be impressed by this demonstration, and sets his watch accordingly.

Before he leaves, Bob says to the patient, "That was really quite remarkable, but tell me, what do you do on a cloudy day, or at night, when the stick casts no shadow?" The patient holds up his wrist and says, "I suppose I would just look at my watch."

PERSONAL TRAINING

For my fiftieth birthday, my wife purchased a week of personal training at the health club for me. Although I am still in great shape, I decided it would be a good idea to give it a try, so I called the club and made my reservations with a personal trainer named Belinda, who identified herself as a twenty-five-year-old aerobics instructor and model for athletic clothing and swim wear. My wife seemed pleased with my enthusiasm to get started. The club encouraged me to keep a diary to chart my progress.

MONDAY

Started my day at 6:00 a.m. Tough to get out of bed, but found it was well worth it when I arrived at the health club to find Belinda waiting for me. She is something of a Greek goddess with blond hair, dancing eyes, and a dazzling white smile. Woo Hoo! Belinda gave me a tour and showed me the machines. She took my pulse after five minutes on the treadmill. She was alarmed that my pulse was so fast, but I attribute it to standing next to her in her Lycra aerobic outfit. I enjoyed watching the skillful way in which she conducted her aerobics class after my workout today. Belinda was encouraging as I did my sit-ups, although my gut was already aching from holding it in the whole time she was around. This is going to be a fantastic week.

TUESDAY

I drank a whole pot of coffee, but I finally made it out the door. Belinda made me lie on my back and push a heavy iron bar into the air and then she put weights on it. My legs were a little wobbly on the treadmill, but I made the full mile. Belinda's rewarding smile made it all worthwhile. I feel great! It's a whole new life for me.

WEDNESDAY

The only way I can brush my teeth is by laying the toothbrush on the counter and moving my mouth back and forth over it. I believe I have a hernia in both pectorals. Driving was OK as long as I didn't try to steer or stop. I parked on top of a GEO in the club parking lot. Belinda was impatient, insisting that my screams bothered other club members. Her voice is a little too perky this early in the morning; especially when she scolds me and gets this annoyingly nasally whine.

My chest hurt when I got on the treadmill, so Belinda put me on the stair monster. Why the hell would anyone invent a machine to simulate an activity rendered obsolete by elevators? Belinda told me it would help me get in shape and enjoy life. She said some other crap too.

THURSDAY

Belinda was waiting for me with her vampire-like teeth exposed as her thin, cruel lips were pulled back in a full snarl. I couldn't help being a half an hour late. It took me that long to tie my shoes.

Belinda took me to work out with dumbbells. When she was not looking, I ran and hid in the men's room. She sent Lars to find me. Then, as punishment she put me on the rowing machine, which I sank.

FRIDAY

I hate that bitch Belinda more than any human being has ever hated any other human being in the history of the world. She's a stupid, skinny, anemic little cheerleader. If there was a part of my body I could move without unbearable pain, I would beat her with it. Belinda wanted me to work on my triceps. I don't have any triceps. If you don't want dents in the floor, don't hand me the goddamned barbells or anything that weighs more than a sandwich. The treadmill flung me off and I landed on a health and nutrition teacher.

SATURDAY

Belinda left a message on my answering machine in her grating, shrilly voice wondering why I did not show up today. Just hearing her made me want to smash the machine. However, I lacked the strength to even use the TV remote and ended up watching eleven straight hours of the Weather Channel.

SUNDAY

I'm having the Church van pick me up for services today so I can go and thank God that this week is over. I will also pray that next year my wife, the bitch, will choose a gift for me that is fun, like a root canal.

DENTURES

A couple of old guys were golfing one day, when one of the men said that he was going to go to Doctor Irv Becker for a new set of dentures later that afternoon.

His elderly friend, Charlie Reid remarked that he too had gone to the same dentist a few years before.

"Is that so?" the first old gentleman asked. "Did he do a good job with your dentures?"

Charlie replied, "Well, I was on the course yesterday when someone on the ninth hole hooked a shot. The ball must have been going at least two hundred miles an hour when it hit me right in the testicles."

The first old guy was confused and asked, "I don't understand. What does that have to do with your dentures?"

Charlie answered, "I'll tell you my friend. That was the first time in two years that my teeth didn't hurt."

SPERM INSTRUCTIONS

The newly born sperm was receiving instructions in conception from the instructor, “As soon as you hear the siren, run for the tunnel, and swim in a straight line until you get to the entrance of a damp cavern. At the end of the cavern you will find a red, sticky ball which is the egg.

Address the egg and say, ‘I am a Sperm.’ She will answer, ‘I’m the Egg.’ From that moment on you will work together to create the embryo. Do you understand?”

The sperm nodded affirmatively and the instructor said, “OK, good luck.”

Two days later, the sperm is taking a nap when he hears the siren. He immediately heads to the tunnel. Multitudes of sperm swim behind him. He knows he has to arrive first.

When he nears the entrance to the cavern, he looks back and sees that he is far ahead of the other sperm. He is able to swim at a slower pace, but does approach the red sticky ball.

When he finally reaches the red sticky ball, he smiles and says, “Hi, I am a sperm.”

The red sticky ball smiles and says, “Hi, I’m a tonsil.”

PHYSICIAN'S WIFE

A doctor and his wife were sitting over dinner one evening discussing the death of a patient about their own age.

After some thought, the young wife asked her husband if he would remarry if a similar fate would happen to her.

He immediately replied, "Sure I would, honey. You know I don't do well on my own."

"I wouldn't want you to be lonely," replied the wife, "So I guess that's all right."

After a few minutes of contemplation she asked, "So if you were to remarry, would you live in this same house with your new wife?"

"Now that's a silly question," replied the husband, "You know how long it took us to find a suitable house close to the hospital."

She then asked, "Would you sleep in our bed with her?"

"With my back problem, I couldn't even think of getting a different bed."

Then she asked, "Would you let her wear my mink coat?"

He replied curtly, "I paid nine grand for that coat. I sure wouldn't let it collect dust in the closet."

Finally, she asked, "Surely you wouldn't let her use my golf clubs?"

Without hesitation he replied, "Of course not, she's left-handed. . . Oops! Damn!"

SYMPTOMS

One day Tom Knudsen noticed that he had a red ring around his penis, so he went to the doctor.

The doctor gives the guy some cream and said, “If it doesn’t work, come back again tomorrow.”

Tom went back to the doctor and said, “The cream you gave me didn’t work.”

So the doctor gave him a different cream and said, “If that doesn’t work, come back again tomorrow.”

The next day, Knudsen came back to the doctor and said, “This stuff you gave me doesn’t work either.”

So the doctor gave him some more cream and said, “If the red ring is still there when you wake up, come back.”

Next day Tom called the doctor and said, “The cream you gave me worked what was it this time?”

The doctor said, “Nothing special. This time I gave you lipstick remover.”

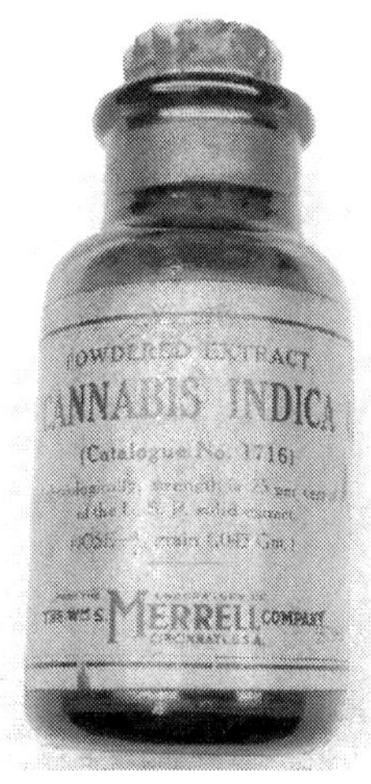

STD

A young man picked up a young girl at a dance. After they danced, the guy said, “I would take you to my house, but my parents are home.”

The girl replied, “I would let you come to my house, except my boyfriend is there.”

He finally suggested that they go to his van.

She agreed and they went to the van. They both took off their clothes, and at the point where the man was about to enter her, the woman exclaimed, “What, no foreplay? How about going outside and look for a stick, and you could beat me with it.”

The man went outside, but couldn’t find any sticks, so he busted the aerial off his van, and the guy and girl beat each other on the back and they had a great time.

The next morning however, the man was feeling very sore on his back and his butt.

He went to his doctor, and the doc exclaimed, “This is the worst case of van-aerial disease I have ever seen.”

BLINDNESS

A pastor, a doctor, and a consultant were waiting for a particularly slow group of golfers.

The consultant fumed, “What’s going on? We must have been waiting for fifteen minutes.”

The doctor chimed in, “I don’t know, but I have never seen such ineptitude.”

The pastor said, “Here comes the greens keeper. Let’s ask him.”

“Hi George, what’s with that group ahead of us? They are rather slow, aren’t they?”

George replied, “Oh yes, that’s a group of blind fire-fighters. They lost their sight saving our clubhouse from a fire last year, so we always let them play for free anytime.”

The group was silent for a moment.

The pastor said, “That is so sad. I think I will say a special prayer for them tonight.”

The doctor said, “Good idea, and I’m going to contact my ophthalmologist buddy and see if there’s anything he can do for them.”

The consultant said, “Why can’t these guys play at night?”

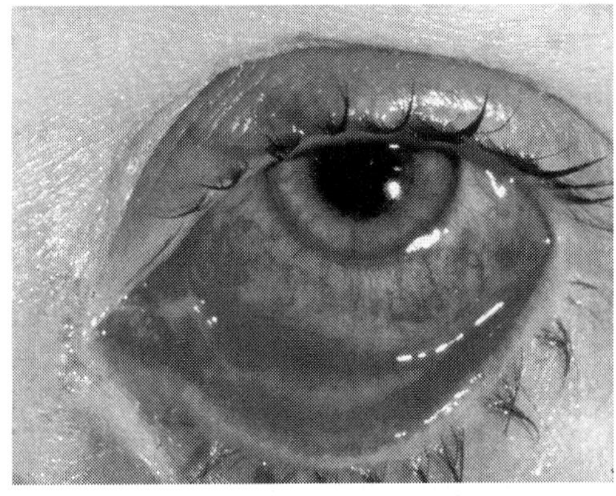

PSYCHIATRIC CHRISTMAS CAROLS

Schizophrenia - Do you Hear What I Hear?

Multiple Personality Disorder - We Three Queens Disoriented Are

Dementia - I Think I'll be Home for Christmas

Narcissistic - Hark the Herald Angels Sing about Me

Manic - Deck the Halls and Walls and House and Lawn and Streets and Stores and Office and Town and Cars and Busses and Trucks and Trees and Fire Hydrants and. . .

Paranoid - Santa Claus is Coming to Get Me.

Personality Disorder - You Better Watch Out, I'm Gonna Cry, I'm Gonna Pout, Maybe I'll tell you why. . .

Borderline Personality Disorder - Thoughts of Roasting on an Open Fire. . .

Obsessive-Compulsive - Jingle Bell, Jingle Bell, Jingle Bell Rock, Jingle Bell, Jingle Bell, Jingle Bell Rock, Jingle Bell, Jingle Bell, Jingle Bell Rock, Jingle Bell, Jingle Bell, Jingle Bell Rock, Jingle Bell, Jingle Bell, Jingle Bell Rock, Jingle Bell, Jingle Bell, Jingle Bell Rock . . .

ARTIFICIAL INSEMINATION

A blonde, Texas, city girl marries a Texas rancher.

One morning, on his way out to check the cows, the rancher says to her, "The artificial insemination man is coming over to impregnate one of our cows today. I drove a nail into the two-by-four just above the cow's stall in the barn. You show him where the cow is when he gets here."

The rancher leaves for the fields.

After a while, the artificial insemination man arrives and knocks on the front door.

The blonde wife takes him down to the barn. They walk along a long row of cows and she sees the nail and tells him, "This is the one right here."

He was impressed by what he seemed to think just might be another ditzy blonde and asks her, "How do you know this is the cow to be bred?"

"That's simple, by the nail over its stall," She explains.

Then the man asks, "What's the nail for?"

She turns to walk away and says, "I guess it's to hang your pants on."

SUPPOSITORY

A man goes to his doctor to pick up his medicine.

When he gets there, his doctor tells him that he has to administer the pills up his butt, because otherwise he might vomit and lose the full benefit.

The doctor asks the man if he would like him to put the pill in today because it's his first time and after this time his wife can do it.

The man agrees.

The doctor inserts the pill into the man's butt.

The man yells loudly, but the doctor reassures him it might sometimes hurt like that, and sends him on his way.

The next day, his wife puts the pill in for him.

As she is inserting the pill, he screams at the top of his lungs.

She asks him what is wrong, because she tried to insert the suppository in gently.

He turns around and tells her, "I remember when the doctor inserted the pill; he had both hands on my shoulders."

OFF DUTY

One night, Phil and Mary are at a bar downing a few beers. They strike up a conversation and quickly discover that they are both doctors.

After about an hour, Phil says to Mary, "How would you like to come back to my place and sleep with me tonight? No strings attached. It will just be one night of fun."

She agrees and they go back to his place. She goes into the bathroom and starts scrubbing up like she's about to go into the operating room. She scrubs for what seems like twenty minutes.

Finally, she comes into the bedroom and they have sex for a very long time.

Afterwards, Phil says to the woman, "You are an OB GYN, aren't you?"

"Yes, how did you know?"

"I could tell by the way you scrubbed up before we started."

"That makes sense," she says.

"You're an anesthesiologist, aren't you?"

"Yes I am," says Phil. "How did you know?"

She replies, "I didn't feel a thing."

PSYCHIATRY AND PROCTOLOGY

Two doctors opened an office in a small town and put up a sign reading, “Dr. Smith and Dr. Jones, Psychiatry and Proctology.”

The town council was not happy with the sign and wanted something a bit more creative, so the doctors changed it to,

“Hysterias and Posteriors.”

This was not acceptable either, so in an effort to satisfy the council they changed the sign to,

“Schizoids and Hemorrhoids.” No go. Next, they tried,

“Catatonics and High Colonics.” Thumbs down again. Then came,

“Manic Depressives and Anal Retentives.” Still no good.

“Minds and Behinds.” Unacceptable again.

“Lost Souls and Butt Holes.” No way.

“Analysis and Anal Cysts?” Won’t work.

“Nuts and Butts?” Not a chance.

“Freaks and Cheeks?” Not liking this one.

“Loons and Moons?” Forget it.

Almost at their wit’s end, the doctors finally came up with,

“Dr. Smith and Dr. Jones, Odds and Ends.”

It passed.

Emergency Department

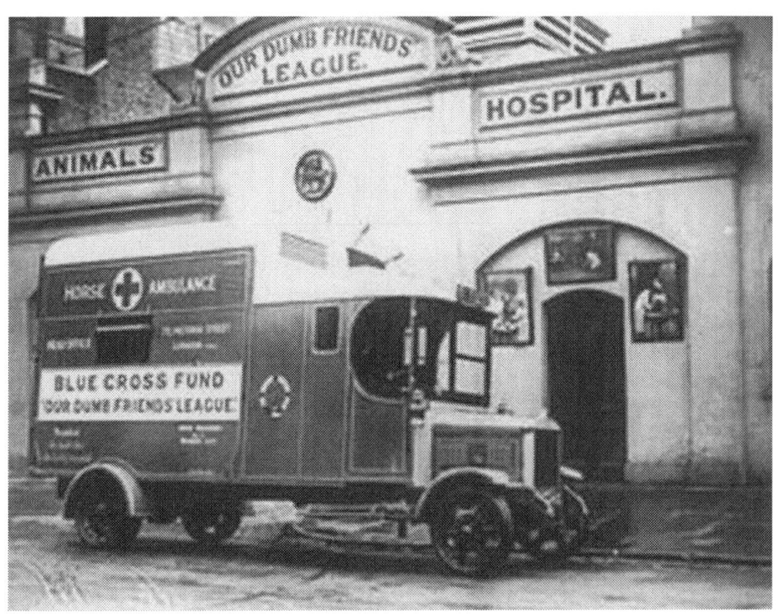

ED CUTTINGS

A rather large woman came in the ED wearing a sweatshirt with 'Guess' on it.

The doctor said, "Thyroid problem?"

✂ ✂ ✂

A medical transcriptionist was typing an ED report that was dictated by a female physician. She was treating a male patient for an erection that wouldn't go down. At the conclusion of the report, the female doctor stated, "The patient was instructed to call me immediately if he should experience another erection over the weekend."

✂ ✂ ✂

The patient presented and the doctor placed a stethoscope on the elderly and slightly deaf female patient's anterior chest wall. "Big breaths," he instructed.

"Yes, they used to be," the patient cooed.

✂ ✂ ✂

✂ ✂ ✂

A woman phoned frantically to her pediatrician late one night, “Doctor, it’s terrible, my two year old baby just ate a condom.”

“Calm down,” says the doctor, “I’m coming over immediately.”

The doctor gets quickly dressed, and is just about to leave the house when the phone rings again.

“Doctor, it’s me again. You don’t need to come over, we found another condom.”

✂ ✂ ✂

A young woman presents to the clinic with a chief complaint of a blue vaginal discharge. Exam revealed blueberries. It appears that she used Blueberry Yogurt as a home treatment for yeast candidiasis.

✂ ✂ ✂

A former radiologist from Northern Ireland tells us that years ago, he was dressed up in lead apron and gloves, and was conducting a radiographic examination of a woman’s abdomen.

Finding that her clothing was causing some opacity on the fluorescent screen, he remarked, “Would you pull down your knickers, please?”

The patient did nothing, so he repeated the request.

He then heard her say, “I’m so sorry, doctor. I thought you were talking to the nurse.”

✂ ✂ ✂

Receptionist: What’s the nature of your emergency?

Caller: My wife is pregnant and her contractions are only two minutes apart

Receptionist: Is this her first child?

Caller: No, you idiot. This is her husband.

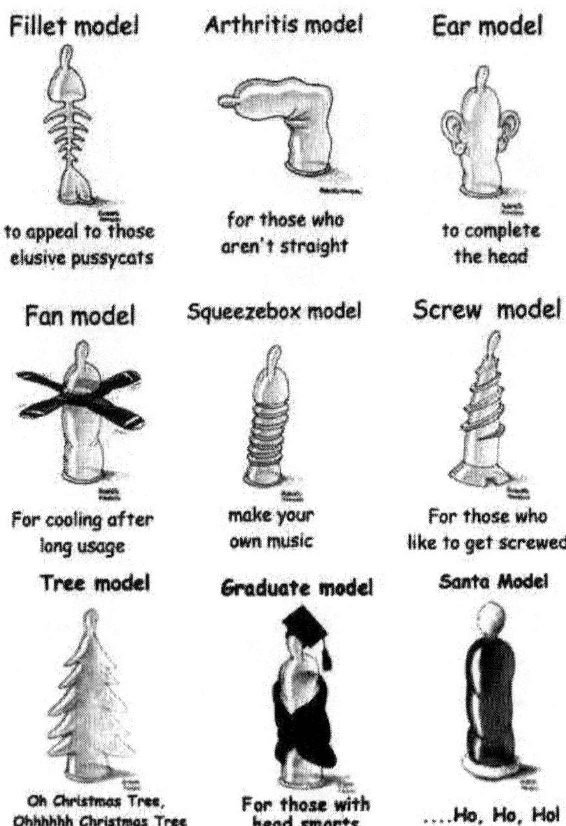

New Condom Models

While visiting his niece, an elderly man had a heart attack. The woman drove wildly to get him to the emergency room.

After what seemed like a very long wait, the ED doctor appeared, wearing his scrubs.

He said, "I'm afraid that your uncle's brain is dead, but his heart is still beating."

"Oh dear," cried the woman. "We never had a Democrat in the family before.

✂ ✂ ✂

A husband and wife are on the ninth green when suddenly she collapses from a heart attack.

"Help me dear," she groans to her husband.

The husband dials 911 on his cell phone, talks for a few minutes, picks up his putter, and lines up his putt.

His wife raises her head off the green and stares at him, "I'm dying over here, and you're putting?"

"Don't worry dear," says the husband calmly. "They found a doctor on the second hole and he's coming to help you."

"Well how long will it take for him to get here," she asks feebly?

"No time at all," says her husband, practicing his putting stroke. "Everybody's already agreed to let him play through."

✂ ✂ ✂

While assisting in an exam on a young woman who came to the ED with lower abdominal pains, the doctor asked her if she was sexually active.

The young woman appeared slightly embarrassed by the question, and replied, "Not really, I usually just lay there."

✂ ✂ ✂

Ole and Lena were out walking and Lena clutched her heart and fell to the sidewalk. Ole got out his cell phone and called 911. The operator asked, "Where are you?"

Ole answered, "We were walking, and Lena is on the sidewalk on Eucalyptus Street."

The operator asked, "How do you spell that?"

The phone seemed to go dead. The operator kept shouting for Ole. She could hear him panting. He finally came back on line and said, "I dragged her over to Oak Street, that's O-A-K."

✂ ✂ ✂

✂ ✂ ✂

A patient who came into the ED by EMS had attempted suicide by slitting his wrists. The ED doctor sewed him up and while working on the patient asked him why he tried to kill himself.

The doctor jokingly told the patient that if he really wanted to kill himself, he needed to use a gun. He then discharged the patient.

Two hours later, the same patient returned after another suicide attempt. He had shot himself with a gun, in the same place where he had slit his wrist only a few hours earlier.

✂ ✂ ✂

One day I had to be the bearer of bad news when I told a wife that her husband had died of a massive myocardial infarct.

Not more than five minutes later, I heard her reporting to the rest of the family that he had died of a massive internal fart.
Dr. Susan Steinberg

✂ ✂ ✂

A man goes into the ED feeling very sick. After a thorough examination the doctor looks up and says, “I have some bad news. You have HAGS.”

“What is HAGS?” the man asks.

“It’s herpes, AIDS, gonorrhea, and syphilis,” says the doctor.

“Oh no.” says the man. “What are you going to do?”

“We are going to put you in an isolated room and feed you pancakes and pizza.”

“Is that going to help me,” says the man.

“No,” says the doctor. “But it’s the only food we can think of that we can slide under the door.”

✂ ✂ ✂

While acquainting myself with a new elderly patient, I asked, “How long have you been bedridden?”

After looking confused she answered, “Why, not for about twenty years, when my husband was alive.”
Dr. Steven Swanson

✂ ✂ ✂

... and finally

● DENMARK: A patient broke wind while having surgery and set fire to his genitals. The 30-year-old man was having a mole removed from his bottom with an electric knife when his attack of flatulence was ignited by a spark. His genitals, which were soaked in surgical spirits, caught fire. The man, who is suing the hospital, said: 'When I woke up, my penis and scrotum were burning like hell. Besides the pain, I can't have sex with my wife.' Surgeons at the hospital in Kjellerups said: 'It was an unfortunate accident.'

✂ ✂ ✂

Diarrhea must be inherited, because it runs in your jeans.

A man went to the ED to have his wedding ring cut off from his penis. According to the nurse, the patient's girl friend found the ring in his pants pocket and she was so angry with him, she used petroleum jelly to slip the ring on his penis while he was asleep.

You decide what's worse:

- Having your girl friend find out you are married.
- Explaining to your wife how your wedding ring got on your penis.
- Finding out your penis fits through your wedding ring.

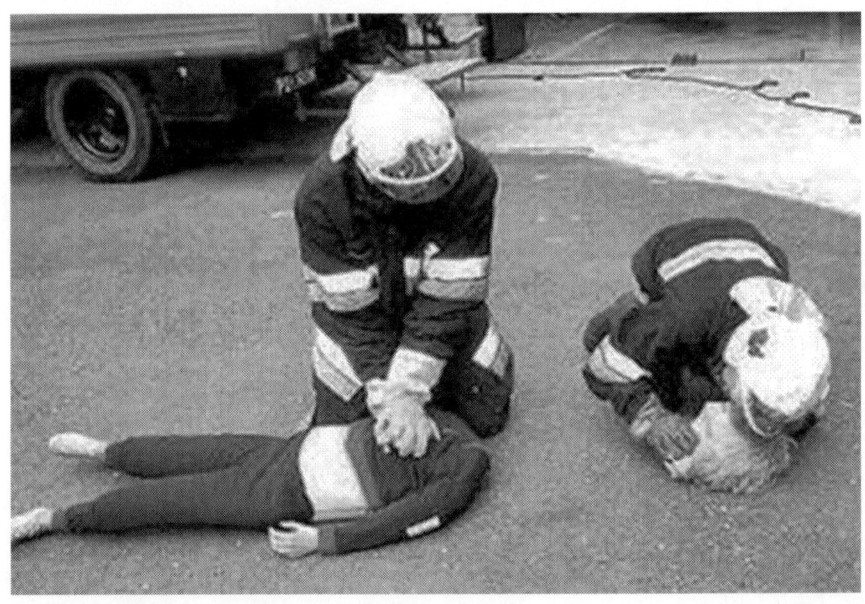

Irish CPR

A man comes into the ED and yells, "My wife's going to have her baby in the cab!" I grabbed my stuff, rushed out to the cab, lifted the lady's dress, and began to take off her underwear.

Suddenly I noticed that there were several cabs, and I was in the wrong one.
Dr. Mark MacDonald

A man was in an accident and his penis was chopped off. He was rushed to the hospital ED where the doctor examined him. After careful examination the doctor said, “We can replace it with a small size for two thousand dollars, a medium size for five thousand dollars, or an extra-large size for ten thousand dollars. I realize it’s a lot of money, so take your time and talk it over with your wife.”

When the doctor came back into the room, he found the man staring sadly at the floor. “We have decided,” the man told him as he choked back tears. “My wife says she would rather have a new kitchen.”

There was a patient in the ED from the pickle factory with an eye injury. The odor of the pickles was quite strong. The doctor treated her eye injury with antibiotics and an eye patch.

As he was giving the patient her discharge instructions, she asked if she could shower to rid herself of the pickle odor.

He replied no, because her eye patch couldn’t get wet.

The blonde patient’s next question was, “How about if I wrap a plastic bag tightly around my head and then shower?”

An old woman, who was particularly despondent over the recent death of her husband, decided that she would just kill herself and join him in death.

Thinking that it would be best to get it over with quickly, she took out his old military pistol and made the decision to shoot herself in the heart since it was so badly broken in the first place.

Not wanting to miss the vital organ and become a vegetable and burden to someone, she called her local hospital to inquire as to just exactly where the heart would be.

The doctor said, “Your heart would be just below your left breast.”

Later that night, she was admitted to the ED with a gunshot wound to her left knee.

I was performing a complete physical, including the visual acuity test. I placed the patient twenty feet from the chart and began, “Cover your right eye with your hand.”

He read the 20/20 line perfectly.

“Now your left.” Again, a flawless read.

“Now both,” I requested. There was silence.

He couldn’t even read the large E on the top line. I turned and discovered that he had done exactly what I had asked; he was standing there with both his eyes covered. I was laughing too hard to finish the exam.
Dr. Matthew Theodropolous

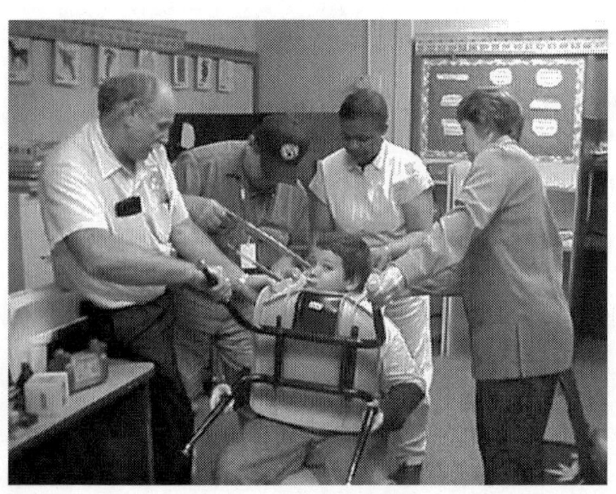

This kid is really stuck

I was caring for a woman from Kentucky and asked, “So how was your breakfast this morning?” “It was very good, except for the Kentucky Jelly. I can’t seem to get used to the taste,” the patient replied.

I asked to see the jelly and the woman produced a packet labeled, “KY Jelly.” Dr. Leonard Kransdorf

A blonde is explaining to her girlfriend the bad day she had at work and that her boss had suffered a heart attack and died.

"That's horrible," says the friend. "What did you do?"

The blonde replies, "There was nothing I could do. He kept yelling at me to call 9-1-1, but he wouldn't tell me the rest of the numbers."

During a patient's two week follow-up appointment with his cardiologist, he informed me that he was having trouble with one of his medications. "Which one?" I asked.

"The patch. The nurse told me to put on a new one every six hours and now I'm running out of places to put it."

I had him quickly undress and discovered what I hoped I wouldn't see. The man had over fifty patches on his body. Now instructions include 'removal of the old patch before applying a new one'. Dr. Rebecca St. Clair

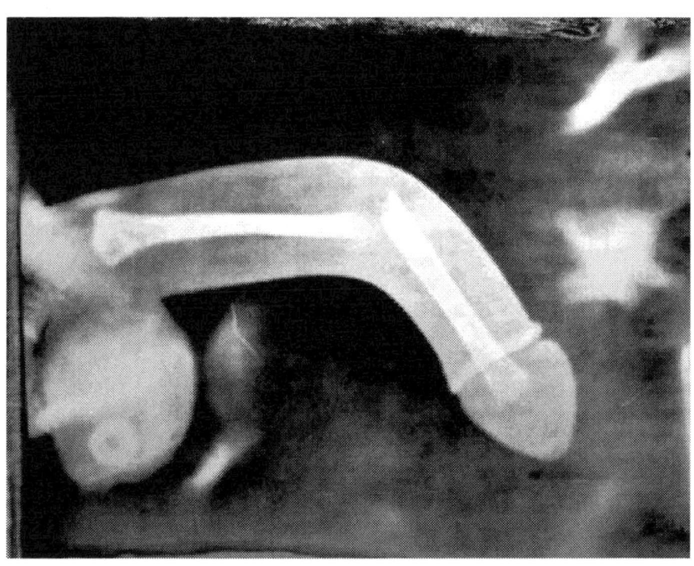

Talk about a broken bone. Ouch!

Darwin winner - In France, a man left nothing to chance when he decided to commit suicide. He stood at the top of a tall cliff and tied a noose around his neck. He tied the other end of the rope to a large rock. He drank some poison and set fire to his clothes. He even tried to shoot himself at the last moment. He jumped and fired the pistol.

The bullet missed him completely and cut through the rope above him. Free of the threat of hanging, he plunged into the sea. The sudden dunking extinguished the flames and made him vomit the poison. He was dragged out of the water by a fisherman, and was taken to a hospital, where he died of hypothermia.

A student at Boston University wavered for some time between a career as a proctologist and a job as a barber. He eventually flipped a coin to see how it came out; heads. . . or tails.

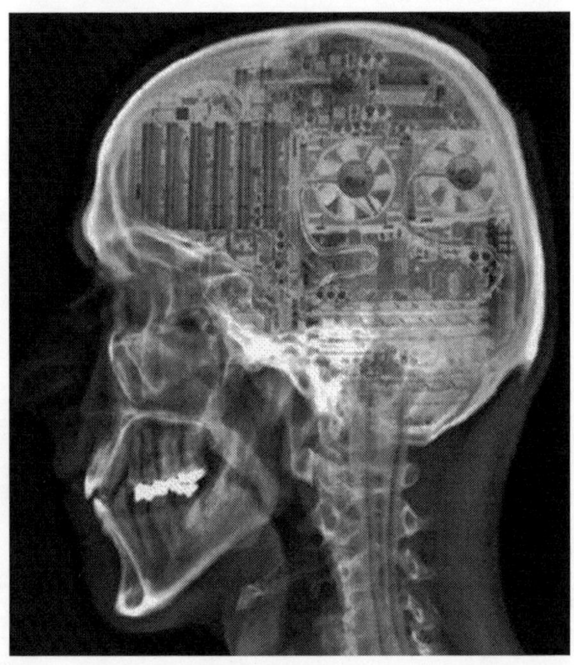

Geek X-ray

A young woman with purple hair, tattoos, and strange clothing, entered the ED. It was quickly determined that the patient had acute appendicitis, so she was scheduled for immediate surgery. On the operating table, the staff noticed that her pubic hair had been dyed green, and above it there was a tattoo that read, "Keep off the grass." Once the surgery was completed, the surgeon wrote a short note on the patient's dressing, which said, "Sorry, had to mow the lawn."

Three paramedics were boasting about improvements in their respective ambulance team's response times.

"Since we installed our new satellite navigation system," bragged the first one, "We cut our emergency response time (ERT) by ten percent."

The other paramedics nodded in approval. "Not bad," the second paramedic commented, "But by using a computer model of traffic patterns, we have cut our average ERT by twenty percent."

Again, the other team members gave their congratulations, until the third paramedic said, "That's nothing, since our ambulance driver passed the bar exam, we cut our emergency response time in half."

I went to the emergency department and since I did not want to sit there for four hours, I put on my old flight jacket and stuck a patch that I downloaded off the Internet onto the front of it.

When I arrived at the ED, I noticed that three quarters of the people got up and left. I guess they decided that they weren't that sick after all. It cut at least three hours off my waiting time.

Here is the patch I used. Feel free to use it if you need quick service.

ED Shift End:

All targets met

All systems working

All customers satisfied

All staff eager and enthusiastic

All pigs fed and ready to fly.

BURNED UP

One morning, a husband and wife were going about their regular morning routine, getting ready for work. The husband was preparing breakfast while the wife was in the bathroom putting on her makeup and fixing her hair.

The nozzle of her hairspray can was clogged, so she ran it under hot water, then test-sprayed it into the toilet. The hairspray can worked fine, so she finished getting ready and went down to enjoy breakfast.

With the bathroom now clear, the husband grabbed his morning paper and his cigarettes, intending to enjoy some quiet time on the toilet.

He lit a cigarette and smoked while he read the sports section, and then dropped the remainder of the cigarette into the toilet.

The lit cigarette came into contact with the hairspray and made for a spectacular light show. The husband's genital area was badly burned.

The wife called 9-1-1 and ambulance personnel arrived. After initial treatment, the attendants were loading the husband's stretcher into the ambulance when the wife told them what had happened.

They were laughing so hard, they dropped the stretcher, and broke his left arm.

ED MEDICAL CODES

ALP – Acute Lead Poisoning (a gunshot wound)

ALP (A/C) – Acute Lead Poisoning (Air Conditioning) (multiple gunshot wounds)

AMF Yo Yo – Adios (You're On Your Own)

ART – Assuming Room Temperature (deceased)

Bagged and Tagged – A body that is ready to be taken to the hospital morgue (it's in a body bag and has a toe tag)

Code Brown – Take a guess!

Code Yellow – A patient who has wet the bed

Code Zero – Another 'Frequent Flyer'. The real radio codes range from Code 1 (not serious) to Code 4 (emergency) *see below*

DFO – Done Fell Out (of bed)

DRT – Dead Right There - Similar to DOA except when we got there, they were Dead Right There

Flower Sign – Lots of flowers at a patient's bedside (may indicate the patient is a good candidate for early discharge, since they have friends and family who can care for them)

FOOSH – Fell Onto Outstretched Hand (a broken wrist)

FORD – Found On Road Dead

Frequent Flyer – Someone who is regularly taken to the hospital in an ambulance, even though they aren't sick (it's free and something to do)

House Red – Blood

Insurance Pain – An inordinate amount of neck pain following a minor auto collision with a wealthy driver

MGM Syndrome – A patient who is faking illness and putting on a really good show

SYB – Save Your Breath (as in, “SYB, he WNL”)

T&T Sign – Tattoos-and-teeth. (Patients with a lot of tattoos and missing teeth are more likely to survive major injuries)

TMB – Too Many Birthdays (suffering from old age)

TRO – Time Ran Out

WNL – Will Not Listen

SUICIDE

A blonde hurries into the emergency room late one night with the tip of her index finger shot off.

“How did this happen?” the emergency room doctor asked her.

“I was trying to commit suicide,” the blonde replied.

“You tried to commit suicide by shooting your finger off?”

“No, silly,” the blonde said, “First I put the gun to my chest and I thought, I just paid six thousand dollars for these breast implants, I’m not shooting myself in the chest.”

“Then,” asked the doctor?

“Then I put the gun in my mouth and I thought, I just paid three thousand dollars to get my teeth straightened, I’m not shooting myself in the mouth.”

“Then what did you do?”

“Then I put the gun to my ear and I thought, “This is going to make a loud noise. So I put my finger in the other ear before I pulled the trigger.”

ACCIDENT

A man was at the country club for his weekly round of golf. He began his round with an eagle on the first hole and a birdie the second. On the third hole he had just scored his first ever hole-in-one when his cell phone rang.

It was a doctor notifying him that his wife had just been in a terrible accident and was in critical condition in the Emergency Department.

The man told the doctor to inform his wife where he was and that the he would be there as soon as possible. As he hung up he realized he was leaving what was shaping up to be his best ever round of golf.

He decided to get in a couple of more holes before heading to the hospital. He ended up finishing all eighteen. He finished his round shooting a personal best sixty-one shattering the club record by five strokes and beating his previous best game by more than ten.

He was jubilant, and then he remembered his wife. Feeling guilty he dashed to the hospital Emergency Department. He saw the doctor in the hall and asked about his wife's condition.

The doctor glared at him and shouted, "You finished your round of golf didn't you? I hope you're proud of yourself. While you were out for the past four hours enjoying yourself at the country club your wife has been languishing in the Emergency Department. It's just as well you went ahead and finished that round because it will be more than likely your last. For the rest of her life she will require around the clock care and you will be her caregiver."

The man was feeling so guilty he broke down and sobbed.

The doctor started to snicker and said, "Just kidding. She died more than two hours ago. What did you shoot?"

LOOKS LIKE. . .

Joe Dougherty staggers into an Emergency Department with a concussion, multiple bruises, two black eyes, and a five iron wrapped tightly around his throat.

Naturally the doctor asks him what happened.

The man said, "I was having a quiet round of golf with Lennie until we approached a very difficult hole. We both sliced our balls into a pasture of cows.

We went to look for them, and while I was rooting around I noticed one of the cows had something white in its rear end. I walked over and lifted up the tail, and there was a golf ball with Lennie's monogram on it. The ball was stuck right in the middle of the cow's butt.

That's when I made my mistake."

"What did you do?" asks the doctor.

I lifted the tail, pointed, and yelled to her, "Hey, Lennie, this one looks like yours."

ANGINA

There is a fire department in Toronto who arrived to a 9-1-1 call for a man from his frantic family members.

When they arrived to the scene, the family members were crowded around the man and were sobbing. After attempting to obtain a history, the fire folks discovered that none of the family members spoke much English.

One of the firefighters pushed the family members aside and began CPR while another administered some oxygen.

Unfortunately, they didn't know that the man had a history of angina and the family had smeared his bare chest with nitro cream. After a few pumps, the firefighter administering compressions passed out.

Still unaware of the nitro, a second firefighter began compressions. He also passed out after just a few compressions.

A third firefighter began compressions after pushing aside the bodies of the previous compressors, and he too fell unconscious.

Finally, the fourth firefighter ended this cycle when he held his hands up in the air and exclaimed, "I'm not touching him."

GIVING BIRTH

It was late at night and Yucky Chucky's mother, who was expecting her second child, was home alone with her young son. When she started going into labor, she dialed 911.

Due to other problems, only one paramedic responded to the call. The house was very dark, so the paramedic asked Chucky to hold a flashlight high over his mom so he could see while he helped deliver the baby.

Very diligently, Chucky did as he was asked. His mother pushed and pushed, and after a little while Tommy was born. The paramedic lifted him by his little feet and spanked him on his bottom.

Tommy began to cry.

The paramedic then thanked Chucky for his help and asked what he thought about the events he had just witnessed.

Chucky responded, "He shouldn't have crawled in there in the first place. Smack him again."

Operating Room

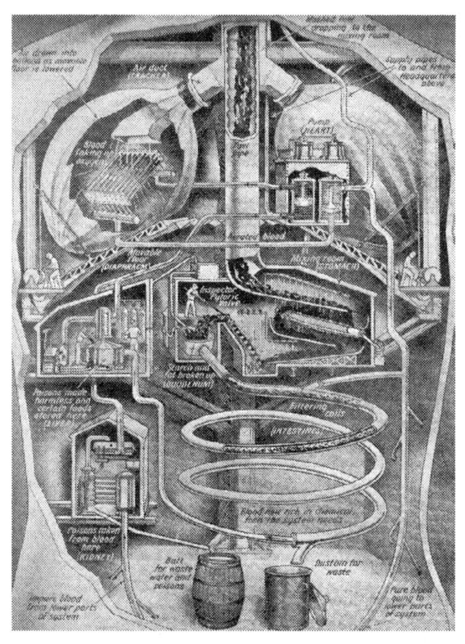

OR STITCHINGS

One bright day in surgery the doctors were preparing a ninety year old women for spinal anesthesia. The anesthesiologist washed her back and, before injecting the local, warned her, "You're going to feel a little prick, now."

She turned and replied, "You'd better be talking about a needle, young man."

Four surgeons were taking a coffee break and discussing their work. The first surgeon said, "I think that accountants are the easiest to operate on. You open them up and everything inside is numbered."

The second surgeon said, "I think that librarians are the easiest to operate on. You open them up and everything is in alphabetical order."

The third surgeon said, "I think that electricians are the easiest to operate on. You open them up and everything is color coded."

The fourth surgeon said, "I think that lawyers are the easiest to operate on. They're heartless, spineless, gutless, and their heads and asses are interchangeable."

ଓ ଓ ଓ ଓ

A man is recovering from surgery when a nurse asks him how he is feeling. "I'm OK, but I didn't like the four-letter-word the doctor used in surgery," he answered.

"What did he say," asked the nurse.

"OOPS!"

ଓ ଓ ଓ ଓ

An older Jewish gentleman was on the operating table awaiting surgery and he insisted that his son, a renowned surgeon, perform the operation.

As he was about to receive the anesthesia, he asked to speak to his son.

"Yes dad, what is it?"

"Don't be nervous son, do your best, and just remember, if it doesn't go well, if something happens to me, your mother is going to come and live with you and your wife."

ଓ ଓ ଓ ଓ

A medical study has found that clowns in an operating room are beneficial to recovery of young patients. . .
The reason is that kids think, "Wow, at least I'm not him."

ଓ ଓ ଓ ଓ

A surgeon went to check on his blonde patient after an operation. She was awake, so he examined her. "You will be fine," he said.

She asked, "How long will it be before I am able to have a normal sex life again doctor?"

The surgeon hesitated.

"What's the matter doctor? I will be all right, won't I?"

He replied, "Yes, you will be fine. It's just that no one has ever asked me that after having their tonsils out."

ශ ශ ශ ශ

A well respected surgeon was relaxing on his sofa one evening just after arriving home from work. As he was tuning into the evening news, the phone rang. The doctor calmly answered it and heard the familiar voice of a colleague on the other end of the line.

"We need a fourth for poker," said the friend.

"I'll be right over," whispered the doctor.

As he was putting on his coat, his wife asked, "Is it serious?"

"Oh yes, quite serious," said the doctor gravely. "In fact, three other doctors are there already."

ශ ශ ශ ශ

After surgery, they put you in the expensive care unit.

ශ ශ ශ ශ

After a grueling operation, the doctor said, "That was a close one. An inch either way and it would have been out of my specialty."

ශ ශ ශ ශ

A Newfie doctor explained to his patient that he had a serious ailment for which an operation was absolutely imperative.

The patient turned pale and asked, "Is it very dangerous?"

"Yes," the doctor replied. "Five out of six who undergo this operation die, but you have nothing to worry about."

"Why not?" inquired the patient.

"You are sure to recover because my last five patients died," the doctor reassured him.

ශ ශ ශ ශ

What's the difference between a surgeon and a puppy?
If you put a puppy in a room by itself for an hour, it'll probably stop whining.

Two gay men decide to have a baby. They mix their sperm, and then have a surrogate mother artificially inseminated.

The surrogate mother goes in and has a C-Section and both mother and baby are fine. She calls the fathers and they rush to the hospital.

She tells them where the nursery is and they see twenty-four babies lying in the nursery. Twenty-three of them are crying and screaming. One calm baby is smiling serenely.

A nurse comes by, and to the gays' delight, she points out the happy child is theirs.

"Isn't it wonderful?" one exclaims. "All these unhappy children and ours is so happy."

The nurse says, "He's happy now. But just wait until we take the pacifier out of his butt."

Two little kids are in a hospital, lying on stretchers next to each other, outside the operating room.

The first kid leans over and asks, "What are you in here for?"

The second kid says, "I'm in here to get my tonsils out, and I'm a little nervous."

The first kid says, "You've got nothing to worry about. I had that done when I was four. They put you to sleep, and when you wake up they give you lots of Jell-O and ice cream. It's a breeze."

The second kid then asks, "What are you here for?"

The first kid says, "A circumcision."

The second kid says, "Whoa, good luck buddy, I had that done when I was born and couldn't walk for a year.

HEART SURGEON

A mechanic was removing a cylinder head from the motor of a Harley when he spotted a famous heart surgeon in his shop. The surgeon was waiting for the service manager to come look at his bike.

The mechanic shouted across the garage, "Hey doc, can I ask you a question?"

The surgeon was a bit surprised, but walked over to the mechanic working on the motorcycle.

The mechanic straightened up, wiped his hands on a rag, and asked, "Doc, look at this engine, I can open it up, take valves out, fix them and put in new parts, and when I finish, this will work just like a new one. What I don't understand is why I get such a pittance and you get the really big money when you and I are doing basically the same work?"

The surgeon paused, smiled, leaned over, and said, "Try doing it with the engine running."

THINGS YOU DO NOT WANT TO HEAR IN SURGERY

- Better save that. We will need it for the autopsy.
- Wait a minute, if this is his spleen, then what's that?
- Hand me that. . . uh. . . that uh, sharp thingie.
- Oh no! I just lost my Rolex.
- There go the lights again. . .
- Ya' know there's big money in kidneys and this guy has two.
- Could you stop that thing from beating? It's throwing my concentration off.
- What's this doing here?
- I hate it when they're missing stuff in here.
- Well folks, this will be an experiment for all of us.
- Sterile? The floor's clean, right?
- What do you mean he wasn't in for a sex change?
- OK, now take a picture from this angle.
- This is truly a freak of nature.
- Nurse, did this patient sign the organ donation card?
- Don't worry. I think it is sharp enough.
- Rats! Page fifty of the manual is missing.
- Isn't this the one with the really lousy insurance?

SURGERY

Sam and John were out cutting wood, and John cut his arm off. Sam wrapped the arm in a plastic bag and took it and John to a surgeon.

The surgeon said, "You are in luck. I'm an expert at reattaching limbs. Come back in four hours."

Sam came back in four hours and the surgeon said, "I finished faster than I expected to. John is down at the local pub."

Sam went to the pub and saw John throwing darts.

A few weeks later, Sam and John were out again, and John cut his leg off. Sam put the leg in a plastic bag and took it and John back to the surgeon.

The surgeon said, "Legs are a little tougher. Come back in six hours."

Sam returned in six hours and the surgeon said, "I finished early. John is down at the soccer field."

Sam went to the soccer field and there was John, kicking goals.

A few weeks later, John had a terrible accident and cut his head off. Sam put the head in a plastic bag and took it and the rest of John to the surgeon.

The surgeon said, "Gee, heads are really tough. Come back in twelve hours."

Sam returned in twelve hours and the surgeon said, "I'm sorry, John died."

Sam said, "I understand that heads are tough, but what happened?"

The surgeon said, "The surgery went fine. John suffocated in that plastic bag."

MINOR OPERATION

A beautiful young girl was about to undergo a minor operation. She lay on a rolling bed and the nurse brought her into the corridor.

Before entering the room, the nurse left her behind the Surgery Room door to go in and check if everything was ready.

A man wearing a white coat approached, took the sheet away, and began examining her naked body. He walked away and talked to another man in a white coat.

The second man, Gary Brock, came over and did the same examination.

When a third man, David, started examining her body very closely, she grew impatient and asked, “These examinations are fine and appreciated, but when are you going to start the operation?”

David Muntz shrugged his shoulders and told her, “I have no idea. We are just here reviewing the new wireless network.”

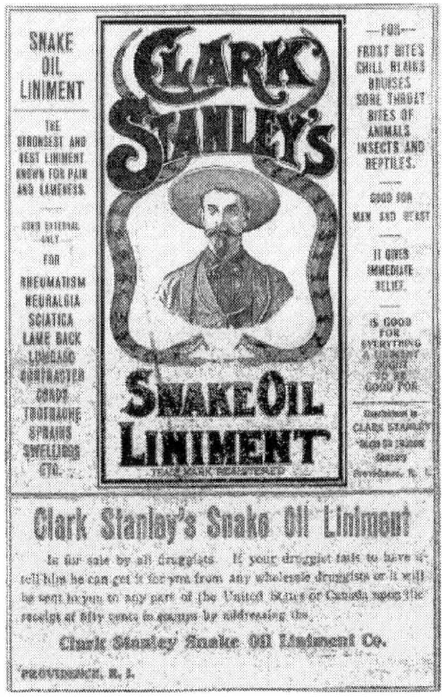

COLONOSCOPIES

A physician claims these are actual comments from his patients made while he was performing Colonoscopies.

"Take it easy, doc. You are boldly going where no man has gone before."

"Find Amelia Earhart yet?"

"Can you hear me now?"

"Oh boy, that was sphincterrific."

"Are we there yet? Are we there yet? Are we there yet?"

"You know, in Arkansas we are now legally married."

"Any sign of the trapped miners, chief?"

"You put your left hand in, you take your left hand out. You do the Hokey Pokey. . ."

"Hey, now I know how a Muppet feels."

"If your hand doesn't fit, you must acquit."

"Hey doc, let me know if you find my dignity."

"You used to be an executive at Enron, didn't you?"

"Could you write me a note for my wife, saying that my head is not, in fact, up there?"

EYE OPERATION

One day, a man had an accident at work, which resulted in him getting his eye gouged out. He was rushed to hospital, and, after awaking from his operation, was told by the doctor that he was given a glass eye.

The man looked in the mirror to see the result, and was shocked to see that his original eye color was blue and his new glass eye was brown. The man was outraged. "I can't walk around like this."

"Sir," the doctor said, "There is a severe shortage of blue eyes. We had to give you a brown one. If you can get a blue eye, and bring it here to the hospital, we will happily fit it for you."

A few weeks later, the man was driving home from work late one night during a big storm. Suddenly, the car in front of him lost control and skidded off the road before finally hitting a tree. The man screeched to a halt, and ran down the embankment to see if he could help. He found the driver of the car sprawled out over the wreckage, dead as a doornail. . . with a blue glass eye.

Because it was so late at night and during such a big storm, no one was around, so the man proceeded to get a tool and remove one of the deceased man's blue eyes, replacing it with his brown glass eye. He raced down to the local hospital to have the replacement blue eye fitted.

A few days later, the man was driving along the same stretch of road when he saw the police examining the crash scene and towing the car wreck away. He was concerned to find out if the police were on to him and decided to go over to see if they had any leads.

"Excuse me, sir," said the policeman, "Do you know anything about this at all?"

"No officer, why do you ask?" said the man.

"We can't figure this out. Somehow, this fellow managed to drive forty miles with two glass eyes."

TESTICLE MISHAP

Based on a bet with the other members of his threesome, Jim Brady tried to wash his own testicles in a ball washer at the local golf course.

Proving once again that beer and testosterone are a bad mix, Jim managed to straddle the ball washer and dangle his balls in the machine.

Much to his dismay, one of his buddies, Brad upped the ante by spinning the crank on the machine with Brady's balls in place, thus wedging them solidly in the mechanism.

Brady immediately passed his threshold of pain, collapsed and tumbled from his perch. Unfortunately for him, the height of the ball washer was more than a foot higher off the ground than his testicles are in a normal stance, and his balls were the weakest link.

His balls ripped open during the fall, and one testicle was plucked from him forever and remained in the ball washer, while the other testicle was compressed and flattened as it was pulled between the housing of the washer, and the rotating machinery inside.

To add insult to injury, Brady broke a new three hundred dollar driver that he had just purchased from the pro shop, and was using to balance himself.

He was rushed to the hospital for surgery, and the remaining guys were asked to leave the course.

A SURGEON'S POEM

We praise the Colorectal Surgeon
Misunderstood and much maligned;
Slaving away in the heart of darkness
Working where the sun don't shine.

We respect the Colorectal Surgeon
Miss a calling you would crave
Lift up your hands and join us
Let's all do the finger wave.

When it comes to spreading joy there are many techniques -
Some spread joy to the world, and others just spread cheeks;
Some may think the cardiologist is their best friend -
But the Colorectal Surgeon knows, he'll get you in the end.

Why be a Colorectal Surgeon?
It's one of those mysterious things
Is it because in natural prescience
There are always openings?

When I first met a Colorectal Surgeon
He did not quite understand
I said, "Hey, it's nice to meet you, but do you mind
we don't shake hands."

He sailed right through medical school because he was a whiz
Oh, but he never thought of psychology though he read passage
A doctor he once had to be, for golf he loved to play
But this is not quite what he meant, by 18 holes a day.

We praise the Colorectal Surgeon
Misunderstood and much maligned;
Slaving away in the heart of darkness
Working where the sun don't shine.

PLASTIC SURGERY

A woman in her forties went to a plastic surgeon for a face-lift.

The doctor told her of a new procedure called, 'The Knob'. A small knob is planted on the back of woman's head and it can be turned to tighten up the skin to produce the effect of a brand new facelift whenever the previous one begins to sag.

The woman chose to get the procedure.

Fifteen years later, she went back to the surgeon. "All these years everything has been working just fine," the woman began, "I had to turn the knob on a number of occasions, and I have always loved the results."

"I'm glad it's been so successful for you," beamed the surgeon.

"Recently however, I have developed two annoying problems. First, I have these terrible bags developing under my eyes, and the knob won't get rid of them."

The doctor looked at her closely and said, "Those aren't bags. Those are your breasts."

"I guess that explains the goatee," she replied.

POLITICAL SURGERY

Three Arkansas surgeons were playing golf together and discussing surgeries they had performed.

One of them said, “I’m the best surgeon in Arkansas. A concert pianist lost seven fingers in an accident, I reattached them, and eight months later he performed a private concert for the Queen of England.”

The second said, “That’s nothing. A young man lost an arm and both legs in an accident, I reattached them, and two years later he won a gold medal in field events in the Olympics.”

The third surgeon said, “You guys are amateurs. Several years ago a lady was high on cocaine and marijuana and she rode a horse head-on into a train traveling eighty miles an hour. All I had left to work with was the horses blond mane and a big ass. Now she is a prominent Senator from New York and was almost nominated as President elect.”

THINGS YOU DON'T WANT TO HEAR WAKING UP AFTER SURGERY

"I don't know what it is, but hurry up and pack it in ice."

"Hey Charlie, unzip the bag on that one, he's still moving."

"Blink once for yes."

"What do you mean we have the wrong patient?"

"Why is there a tag on his toe?"

"Do you think he can hear us?"

"I didn't even know a human could bend that way."

"I'm sorry, we must not have used enough anesthesia. Just relax now.

We'll be done in a jiffy."

"Hold the patient still, we've almost pried it open."

"Did the doctor know he would look like that afterward?"

"Of course I've performed this operation before, nurse."

"Nurse, make sure you're getting all this down. It'll make a great 'ER' script."

AROUND THE WARDS

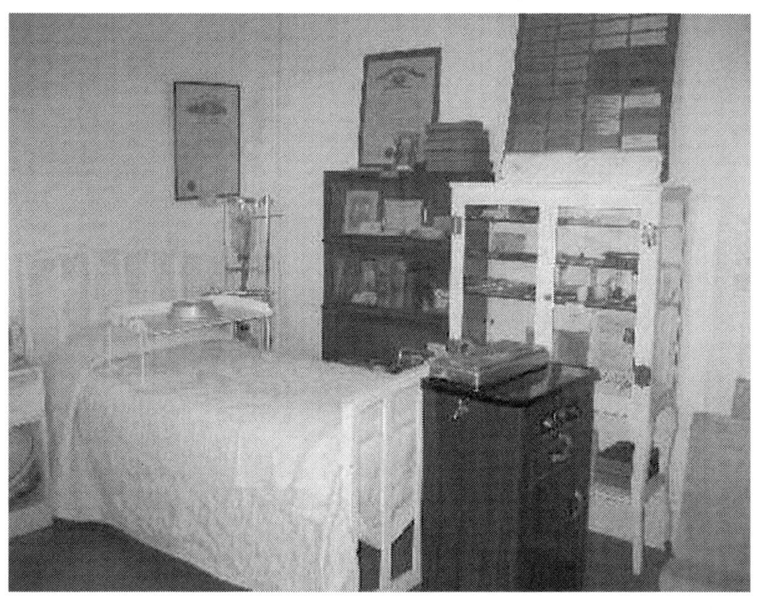

QUICKIES IN BED

Clinophobia: An abnormal and persistent fear of going to bed. Sufferers from clinophobia experience anxiety even though they realize that going to bed normally should not threaten their well-being.

For those in the business, consultants are still trying to determine which is easier, herding cats or implementing CPOE.

Su Wong marries Lee Wong. The next year, the Wongs have a new baby. The nurse brings over a lovely, healthy, but definitely a Caucasian, baby boy.

“Congratulations,” says the nurse to the new parents. “Mr. Wong, what will you and Mrs. Wong name the baby?”

After taking one look, the father realizes a big mistake has been made, but, he is able to see the humor in the situation and decides to make light of it. As he looks at his alleged new son, he says, “Two Wongs don’t make a white, so I think we will name him. . . Sum Ting Wong.

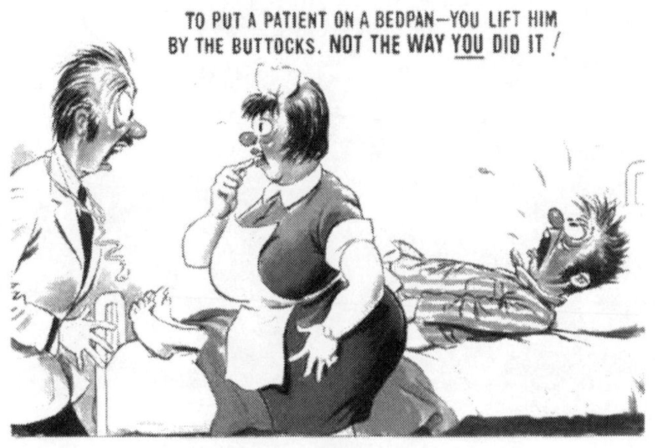

An American teenager was in the hospital bed recovering from serious head wounds received from an oncoming train. When asked how he received the injuries, the lad told police that he was simply trying to see how close he could get his head to a moving train before he was hit.

A proud new father looked at his new son in the hospital nursery, but was lamenting to himself, "With those small arms, you'll never be a weight lifter. With those small legs, you'll never be a dancer. With those tiny eyes, you'll never become a famous astronomer. Oh goodness, you'll never become a porn star, either."

One day three baby boys were born in the hospital at the same time and the nurses mixed them up. They were Jewish, Polish, and German. Everyone stood around wondering how to sort them out.

The German father stepped forward, clicked his heels, and shouted, "Achtung." The German baby jumped up, threw his hand in the air, and replied, "Seig Heil."
The Jewish baby crapped in his diapers, and the Polish baby played in it.

Do you remember way back, when a dope peddler was what we called a stork that delivered stupid babies?

We must always keep in mind the famous saying, "A watched boil never pops"

A nurse was showing some student nurses through the hospital. "This will be the most hazardous section in the hospital for you. The men on this floor are almost well."

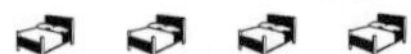

A man falls asleep on the beach under the mid-day sun and suffers severe sunburn to his legs. He's taken to hospital and by the time he gets there his skin has turned bright red. Anything that touches his legs causes him tremendous pain.

The doctor takes a long look at him and then prescribes intravenous feeding of water and electrolytes, a mild sedative, and Viagra.

The nurse is confused and asks, "What good will Viagra do him in that condition?"

"Simple," replies the doctor, "It will keep the sheet off his legs."

A pessimist's blood type is always b-negative.

There was a middle-aged couple that had two stunningly beautiful teenage daughters. The couple decided to try one last time for the son they always wanted.

After months of trying, the wife finally became pregnant and delivered a healthy baby boy.

The joyful father rushed into the nursery to see his new son. He took one look and was horrified to see the ugliest child he had ever seen. He went to his wife and told her there was no way he could be the father of that child.

"Look at the two beautiful daughters I fathered."

Then he gave her a stern look and asked, "Have you been fooling around on me?"

The wife smiled sweetly and said, "Not this time."

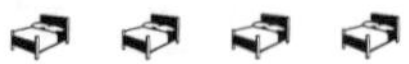

HOW TO PREPARE FOR THE HOSPITAL

Drink a quart of Sherwin-Williams Eggshell One-Coat Coverage Interior Flat White. Then have your child stuff a slinky down your throat.

Put a real estate agent's 'Open House' sign on your front yard and lie on your bed dressed in a paper napkin with straws stuck up your nose.

Put your hand down the garbage disposal while practicing your smile and repeating, "Mild discomfort."

Set your alarm to go off every ten minutes from ten PM to seven AM, at which times you will alternately puncture your wrist with a screwdriver and stab yourself with a knitting needle.

Remove all real food from the house.

With several strands of Christmas lights strung from a coat tree and around yourself, walk slowly up and down the hall pushing the coat tree.

Practice urinating into an empty lipstick tube.

HEALTHSPEAK

A girl walked up to the information desk of a hospital and said, “I’d like to see an upturn.” “Don’t you mean an intern?” asked the nurse.

“I guess I do. I want a contamination.”

“You mean examination,” said the nurse.

“I guess so. I need to go to the fraternity ward,”

“You mean the maternity ward, my dear,” replied the nurse.

The girl loudly replied, “Upturn, intern, contamination, examination, fraternity ward, maternity ward, what’s the difference?

All that I know is that I haven’t demonstrated in two months and I think that I’m stagnant.”

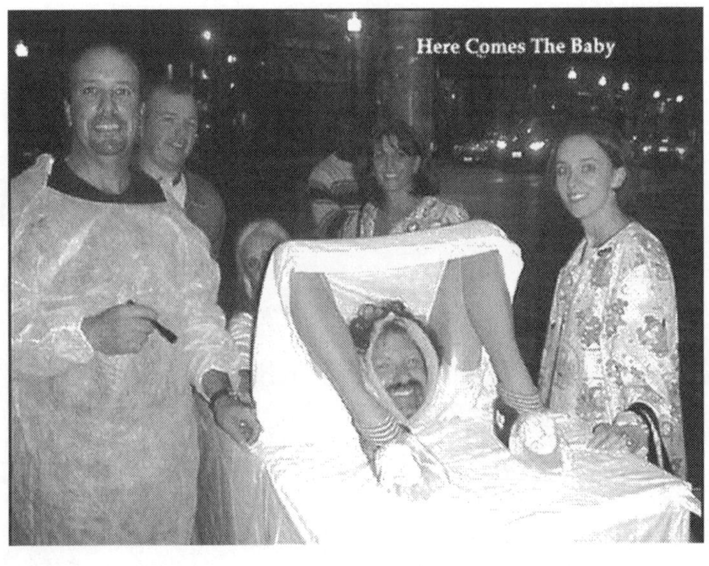

PROFESSOR BONK

Introductory Chemistry at Duke has been taught for many years by Professor Bonk, and his course is semi-affectionately known as 'Bonkistry'. One year there were two students who were taking Chemistry and who did pretty well on all of the quizzes, midterms, labs, etc., and going into the final, they had a solid A.

These two friends were so confident that the weekend before finals, they decided to go party with some friends. They did this and had a great time.

However, with their hangovers, they overslept all day Sunday and didn't make it back until early Monday morning.

Rather than take the final then, they found Professor Bonk after the final and explained to him why they missed the final. They told him that they went away for the weekend, and had planned to come back in time to study, but that they had a flat tire on the way home and didn't have a spare, and couldn't get help for a long time, so were late getting back to campus.

Bonk thought this over and then agreed that the two students could make up the final on the following day. The students were elated and relieved.

They studied that night and went in the next day at the time that Bonk had told them. He placed them in separate rooms and handed each of them a test booklet and told them to begin.

They looked at the first problem, which was easy, and was worth five points. "Cool," they thought, "This is going to be easy." They finished the answer and turned the page.

They were unprepared for what they saw on that page. It read: (95 points) Which Tire?

CARDIAC CARE UNIT

Two patients were in adjacent beds in the Cardiac Care Unit.

One patient asked the other about the purpose of the cardiac monitors, which continually beeped at a steady rate: beep, beep, beep, beep. . .

"I don't know their exact purpose," replied the second patient. "It has something to do with your heart beat. We can ask the doctors about it in the morning."

That night, however, the second patient had a massive cardiac arrest. The cardiac monitor began beeping loudly and quickly.

Some doctors and nurses rushed into the room and began to administer prolonged CPR; at first punching his chest violently, and ultimately using the paddles. Unfortunately, the patient could not be revived.

The next morning, a new patient was admitted to the same room and asked the first patient, "Hey, what's that thing they hook up to you that keeps going beep, beep, beep?"

"I don't know, but be careful not to break it or the doctors and nurses will come running in here and beat you up."

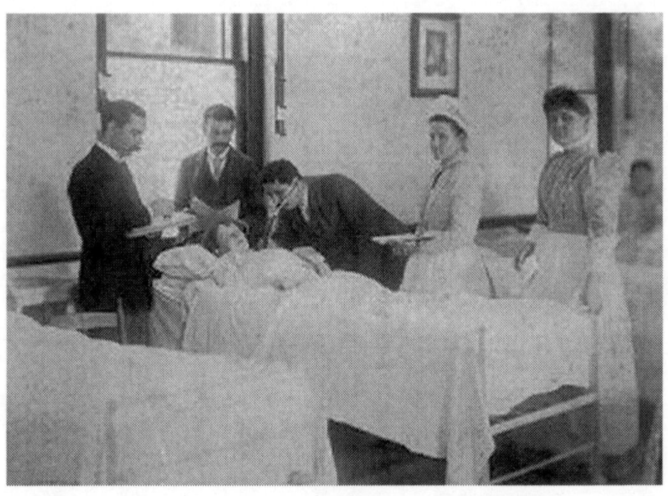

NASTY BUG

A man was sitting at home one evening, when the doorbell rang. When he answered the door, a six-foot tall cockroach was standing there. The cockroach immediately punched him between the eyes and scampered off.

The next evening, the man was sitting at home when the doorbell rang again. When he answered the door, the cockroach was there again. This time, it punched him, kicked him and karate chopped him before running away.

The third evening, the man was sitting at home when the doorbell rang. When he answered the door, the cockroach was there yet again. It leapt at him and stabbed him several times before running off.

The gravely injured man managed to crawl to the telephone and summoned an ambulance.

He was rushed to intensive care, where they saved his life.

The next morning, the doctor was doing his rounds and he asked the man what happened.

The man explained about the six-foot cockroach's attacks, culminating in the near fatal stabbing.

The doctor thought for a moment and said, "Yes, I understand there is a nasty bug going around."

COMA

A man was visiting his wife in hospital where she has been in a coma for several years.

On this visit he decided to rub her left breast instead of just talking to her. When he did this, she let out a sigh.

The man ran out and told the doctor, who said that was a good sign and suggested he should try rubbing her right breast to see if there is any reaction.

The husband went in and rubbed her right breast. This produced another moan from his wife.

He rushed out and told the doctor.

The doctor said this was amazing and a real breakthrough. Then he suggested the man should go in and try oral sex, saying he would wait outside as it is a personal act and he didn't want the man to be embarrassed.

The man went in, and then came out about five minutes later, white as a sheet. He told the doctor his wife was dead.

The doctor asked what happened.

The slightly embarrassed man replied, "I think she choked."

MATERNITY WARD

One very quiet night in the maternity ward, the silence was broken by the sound of a nurse speaking to a young blonde patient. The nurse asked of the blonde if her husband was available.

The blonde replied, “I don’t have a husband.”

The nurse then asked, “How about a boyfriend?”

“No, I’m sorry there’s no one in my life right now.”

The nurse then said, “I have some disturbing news about the baby.”

The blonde gasped, “What is it?”

“Miss, the baby was born black.”

The blonde showed no emotion and replied, “I figured that would happen. You see, I was hard up for money, so I starred in a pornographic film. A black man was the lead.”

The nurse continued, “Well, that’s really none of my business, but you should also know that the baby was born with oriental eyes.”

The blonde replied, “That was the Chinese guy in the movie.”

The nurse continued, “Miss, that’s none of my business, but one last thing, the baby has blonde hair.”

“Oh, that must have been the Swede.”

The nurse was slightly amused by this and went to retrieve the baby. She came into the room and presented the baby to the blonde.

The blonde took the baby in her arms and then suddenly whacked the baby’s bottom. The baby screamed.

The nurse was in shock. “Why did you smack the baby?”

“I just wanted to make sure it didn’t bark.”

DOCTOR'S ORDERS

On a busy Med-Surg floor a doctor stops the nurse to brief her regarding a patient's condition.

"This patient is a fellow physician and my favorite golf partner. His injury is serious and I fear he will not be able to play golf again unless you follow my orders exactly."

The doctor then began listing orders, "You must give an injection in a different location every twenty minutes followed by a second injection exactly five minutes after the first.

He must take two pills at exactly every hour followed by one pill every fifteen minutes for eight hours.

He must drink no more and no less than ten ounces of water every twenty-five minutes and must void between.

Soak his arm in warm water for fifteen minutes then place it in ice for ten minutes and repeat over and over for the rest of the day.

Give range of motion every thirty minutes. He requires a back rub and foot rub every two hours.

Feed him something tasty every other hour. Be cheerful and do whatever he asks at all times.

Chart his condition and vital signs every twenty minutes.

You must do these things exactly as I ordered or his injury will not heal properly, and he will not able to play golf well."

The nurse left the doctor and entered the patient's room. She was greeted by anxious family and an equally anxious patient. All asked the nurse what the doctor had said about the patient.

The nurse started, "The doctor said that you will live." She quickly reviewed the orders and added, "But you will never play golf again."

JOHNSON SYNDROME

Just in case the stress level in your life gets too high, remember you could be working with Johnson.

There was a case in one hospital's Intensive Care Unit where patients always died in the same bed, on Sunday morning at about eleven am, regardless of their medical condition.

This puzzled the doctors, and some even thought that it had something to do with the supernatural. No one could solve the mystery as to why the deaths occurred around eleven am on Sundays.

A World-Wide team of experts was assembled to investigate the cause of the incidents.

The next Sunday morning, a few minutes before eleven am, all doctors and nurses nervously waited outside the ward to see for themselves what the terrible phenomenon was all about.

Some were holding wooden crosses, prayer books, and other holy objects to ward off potential evil spirits.

Just when the clock struck eleven, Mister Johnson, the part-time Sunday janitor, entered the ward and unplugged the life support system so he could use the plug for his vacuum cleaner.

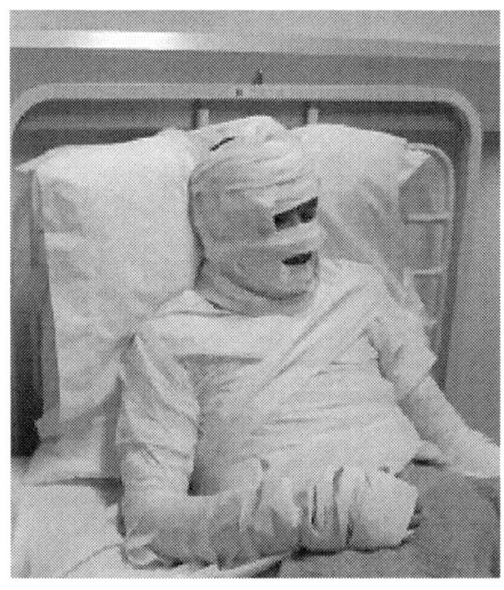

PAIN MANAGEMENT

A married couple went to the hospital to have their baby delivered.

Upon their arrival, the doctor said he had invented a new machine that would transfer a portion of the mother's labor pain to the father of the baby.

He asked if they were willing to try it out. They were both very much in favor of it. The doctor set the pain transfer dial to ten percent for starters, explaining that even ten percent was probably more pain than the father had ever experienced before.

As the labor progressed, the husband felt fine and asked the doctor to go ahead and bump it up a notch. The doctor then adjusted the machine to twenty percent pain transfer.

The husband was still feeling fine. The doctor checked the husband's blood pressure and was amazed at how well he was doing.

At this point they decided to try for fifty percent.

The husband continued to feel quite well. Since it was obviously helping out his wife considerably, the husband encouraged the doctor to transfer all the pain to him.

The wife delivered a healthy baby with virtually no pain. She and her husband were delighted with the results.

When they arrived home, they found the mailman dead on their porch.

WAKING FROM A COMA

A woman's husband had been slipping in and out of a coma for several months, yet she had stayed by his bed side every single day.

One day, he woke up and motioned for her to come closer to him.

She sat by him and he whispered with eyes full of tears, "You know what? You have been with me all through the bad times.

When I got fired, you were there to support me.

When my business failed, you were there.

When I got shot, you were by my side.

When we lost the house, you stayed right here.

When my health started failing, you were still by my side. You know what?"

"What dear?" she gently asked as she smiled and her heart began to fill with warmth.

"I think you are the cause of all my bad luck. Get the heck away from me."

INFORMATION

An old woman calls the hospital and says, “Hello darling. I’d like to talk to the person who gives information regarding your patients. I want to know if the patient is getting better, or doing like expected, or is getting worse.”

Do you know the patient’s name and room number?”

“Yes darling, she is Ellie Morlan in room 302.”

“Oh yes, Ms. Morlan is doing very well. In fact, she’s had two full meals, blood pressure is fine, blood work is normal, and she is going to be taken off the heart monitor in a few hours. If she continues to eat well and to improve, Doctor Whisky will send her home Tuesday afternoon.”

“Thank Goodness. That’s wonderful. That’s fantastic news, darling.”

“From your enthusiasm I take it you must be a close family member or close friend.”

“I am Ellie Morlan in room 302 and Doctor Whisky doesn’t tell me anything.”

Nursing

NURSING NOTES

Did you hear about the nurse who died and went straight to hell?

It took her two weeks to realize she wasn't at work.

Two doctors are in a hospital hallway complaining about Nurse Nancy.

"She's incredibly mixed up. She does everything backward." says one doctor. "Just last week, I told her to give a patient two milligrams of morphine every ten hours. She gave him ten milligrams every two hours. He nearly died on us."

The second doctor says, "That's nothing, earlier this week, I told her to give a patient an enema every twenty four hours. She tried to give him twenty four enemas in one hour. The guy nearly exploded."

Suddenly they hear a bloodcurdling scream from down the hall. "Oh my God," says the first doctor, "I just told her to prick Mister Smith's boil."

Nurse Taylor celebrated her non-existent pay rise with a non-existant Cuban cigar.

A nurse is walking down a hospital corridor when her supervisor spots her.

The supervisor is amazed. The nurse has unkempt hair, her dress is wrinkled, and one of her boobs is hanging out of the front of her uniform.

The nursing supervisor asks, "Nurse Smith, how do you account for standard of dress?"

"Oh," says the nurse, as she pushes her boob back into her uniform. "You know what junior doctors are like. They never put anything back where they find it."

Doctor: Did you take the patient's temperature?
Nurse: No. Is it missing?

A doctor and a nurse just became married. As they were lying in bed one night, the doctor said to his wife, "Honey, to avoid any problems, let's try the following system. When we go to bed at night, if you would like to have sex, pull on my penis one time and if you don't want to have sex, pull on my penis a hundred times."

The nurse was calling on her home-care patient, who was hard of hearing, among other things. She looked at him and said, "You have a suppository in your ear."
"What?" said the man as he cupped his ear.
"You have a suppository in your ear."
"Huh? Speak louder."
After another try, the nurse pulled the suppository out of her patient's ear, pointed to it and said, "You had a suppository in your ear."
"Geez," said the man. "Now I know where I put my hearing aid."

After her hysterectomy, Miss Blondell was given the usual discharge instructions. That night she called, wanting to know if her mother could visit.

"Any time," the nurse replied. "Why do you ask?"

"It says here in your instructions, no relations until after your post-op checkup."

Patient: "Nurse, I just swallowed my pillow."
Nurse: "How do you feel?"
Patient: "A little down in the mouth."

A man was wheeling himself frantically toward the exit of the hospital in his wheelchair, just before his operation.

A nurse stopped him and asked, "What's wrong?"

He said, "I heard the nurse say 'It's a very simple operation, don't worry, I'm sure it will be all right'."

"She was just trying to comfort you, what's so frightening about that?"

"She wasn't talking to me. She was talking to the doctor."

♥ ♥ ♥

How many triage nurses does it take to change a light bulb?

One, but the bulb will have to spend four hours in the waiting room.

A nurse is walking past the hospital staff room, when she hears two African doctors talking. "I'm telling you it's wumba," says the first.

"No. It's woombaa: W-O-O-M-B-A-A," says the second.

"No, no, no. Wumba: W-U-M-B-A," says the first again.

At this the nurse pops her head through the door, "Gentlemen, I think you'll find the word is Womb, W-O-M-B."

The two doctors look blankly at her, and one of them says, "Madam, I doubt if you have ever even seen a water buffalo, let alone heard one fart in a mud pool."

How many doctors does it take to change a light bulb?

Only one, but he has to have a nurse to tell him which end to screw in.

Darren Addy, resided in a nursing home. One day he went into the nurse's office and informed Nurse Monique that his penis died.

Nurse Monique realized that Darren was old and forgetful and decided to play along with him. "It did? I'm sorry to hear that," she replied.

Two days later, Darren was walking down the halls at the nursing home with his penis hanging outside his pants.

Nurse Monique saw him and said, "Mister Addy I thought you told me your penis died."

"It did," he said. "Today is the viewing.

Why did the nurse always insist on using the rectal thermometer to obtain temperatures?

Because nurses are taught in nursing school to always look for her patient's best side.

♥ ♥ ♥

The nurse who can smile when things go wrong is probably going off duty.

They found a dead nurse on the side of the road the other day.
How did they know it was a nurse?
The bladder was full, the stomach was empty, and the backside had been chewed.

Nurses are patient people.

What's the difference between a nurse and a nun?

A nun only serves one God.

A hospital posted a notice in the nurse's lounge saying: "Remember, the first five minutes of a human being's life are the most dangerous." Underneath, a nurse wrote, "The last five are pretty risky, too."

Why did the nurse always insist on using the rectal thermometer to obtain temperatures?

She was taught in nursing school to always look for her patient's best side.

♥ ♥ ♥

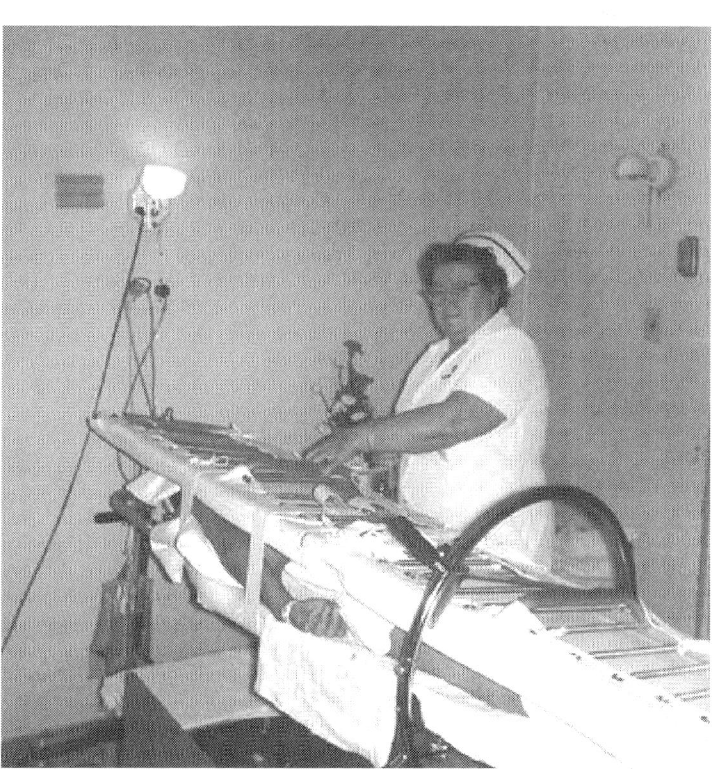

I said I was sorry I called you a name, nurse.

YOU KNOW YOU'RE A NURSE. . .

You know you're a nurse if. . .

- You would like to meet the inventor of the call light some night in a dark alley.
- Your sense of humor gets more warped each year. Almost everything can seem humorous . . . eventually.
- You know the smell of different diarrhea enough to identify it.
- You can tell the pharmacist more about the medication they are dispensing than they know.
- You check the caller id on your day off to see if anyone from the hospital is trying to call and ask you to work.
- You've been telling stories in a restaurant and made someone at another table throw up.
- You notice that you are using more four letter words than you did before you started nursing.
- Every time someone asks you for a pen you can find at least five of them on you.
- You live by the motto, "To be right is only half the battle, to convince the doctor is more difficult."
- You've told a confused patient that your name was that of your coworker and to holler if they need help.
- Your bladder can expand to the size of a Winnebago's water tank.

- Your finger has gone places you never thought possible.
- You have seen more penises than any prostitute. You believe that all bleeding stops. . . eventually.
- Discussing dismemberment over a gourmet meal seems perfectly normal to you.
- Your idea of fine dining is anywhere you can sit down to eat.
- You get an almost irresistible urge to stand and wolf your food even in the nicest restaurants.
- You plan your dinner break whilst lavaging an overdose patient.
- Your diet consists of food that has gone through more processing than most computers.
- You believe chocolate is a food group.
- You refer to vegetables and are not talking about a food group.
- You have the bladder capacity of five people.
- Your idea of a good time is a cardiac arrest at shift change.
- You believe in aerial spraying of Prozac.
- You disbelieve 90% of what you are told and 75% of what you see.
- You have your weekends off planned for a year in advance.
- You encourage an obnoxious patient to sign a self discharge form so you don't have to deal with him any longer.

- Your favorite hallucinogen is exhaustion.
- You believe that ‘shallow gene pool’ should be a recognized diagnosis.
- You believe that the government should require a permit to reproduce.
- You threaten to strangle anyone who even starts to say the “q” word when it is even remotely calm.
- You say to yourself ‘great veins’ when looking at complete strangers at the grocery store.
- You have ever referred to someone’s death as a transfer to the ‘Eternal Care Unit’.
- You have ever wanted to hold a seminar entitled, “Suicide: Doing It Right”.
- You feel that most suicide attempts should be given a free subscription to Guns and Ammo magazine.
- You have ever had a patient look you straight in the eye and say, “I have no idea how that got stuck in there.”
- You have ever had to leave a patient’s room before you begin to laugh uncontrollably.
- You think that caffeine should be available in I/V form.
- You have ever restrained someone and it was not a sexual experience.
- You believe the waiting room should be equipped with a Valium fountain.

- You play poker by betting ectopics on ECG strips.

- You want the lab to perform a 'dumb shit profile'.

- You have been exposed to so many X-rays that you consider radiation a form of birth control.

- You believe that waiting room time should be proportional to length of time from symptom onset.

- Your most common assessment question is "what changed tonight to make it an emergency after 6 hours / days / weeks / months / years)?".

- You have ever had a patient control his seizures when offered some food.

- Your idea of gambling is a blood alcohol level pool instead of a football pool.

- You call subcutaneous emphysema 'Rice Krispies'.

- Your immune system is so well developed that it has been known to attack squirrels in the backyard.

- You recognize that some patients are just dummies.

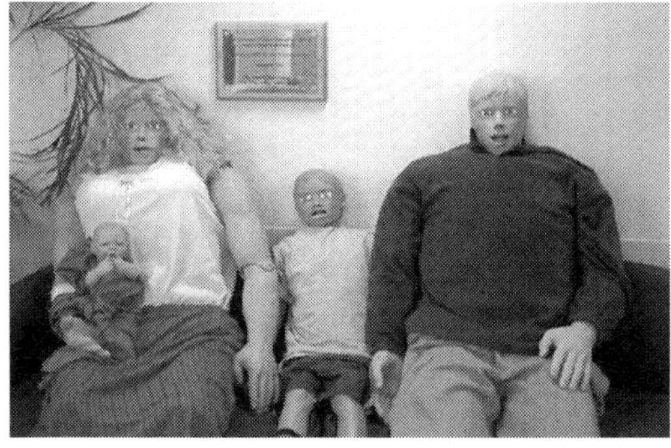

PATIENT PAINS

A big shot businessman had to spend a couple of days in the hospital.

He was a royal pain to the nurses because he bossed them around just like he did his employees. None of the hospital staff wanted to have anything to do with him.

Nurse Robin Raiford was the only one who could stand up to him.

She came into his room and announced, "I have to take your temperature."

After complaining for several minutes, he finally settled down, crossed his arms, and opened his mouth.

"No, I'm sorry," Robin stated, "But for this reading, I cannot use an oral thermometer." This started another round of complaining, but eventually he rolled over and bared his rear end.

After feeling the nurse insert the thermometer, he heard her say, "I have to get something. Now you stay just like that until I get back."

Nurse Raiford leaves the door to his room open on her way out.

He curses under his breath as he hears people walking past his door laughing. After almost an hour, the man's doctor comes into the room.

"What's going on here?" asked the doctor.

Angrily, the man answers, "What's the matter, doc? Haven't you ever seen someone having their temperature taken?"

After a pause, the doctor says, "No, not with a carnation."

TESTICLE CHECK

A man is lying in bed in a Catholic hospital with an oxygen mask over his mouth. A young auxiliary nurse appears to sponge his face and hands.

"Nurse," he mumbles from behind the mask, "Are my testicles black?"

The young nurse replies, "I don't know Mister Jones, I'm only here to wash your face and hands."

He struggles again to ask, "Nurse, Are my testicles black?"

Again the nurse replies, "I can't tell. I'm only here to wash your face and hands."

A nun was passing and saw the man becoming a little distraught so she walked in to inquire what was wrong.

"Sister," he mumbles, "Are my testicles black?"

The sister had been a nurse for many years and was not fazed by the question. She pulled back the bedclothes and pulled down his underwear. She then moved his penis out of the way, had a good look, pulled up his pants, replaced the bedclothes, and announces, "Nothing wrong with them."

At this point, the man pulls off his oxygen mask, looks at the nun, and asks again, "I said, are my test results back?"

RECTUM STRETCHER

A nurse was speeding down the road last week and passed a bridge which had a cop with a radar gun on the other side, laying in wait.

The cop pulled her over, walked up to the car, and asked, "What's your hurry?"

The nurse replied, "I'm late for work."

"Oh yeah," said the cop, "What do you do?"

"I'm a rectum stretcher," she responded.

"A what?" asked the patrolman.

"A rectum stretcher," she repeated.

The cop asked, "Just what does a rectum stretcher do?"

"I start by inserting one finger, then I work my way up to two fingers, then three, then four, then with my whole hand in I work side to side until I can get both hands in. After my both hands are in, I slowly but surely, stretch until it's about six foot wide."

"Just what the hell do you do with a six foot asshole?" asked the cop.

The nurse coolly replied, "You give it a badge, a radar gun, and park him behind a bridge."

SIZES

A male elf was so paranoid about the size of his thingie that he could never work up the courage to have sex. Then one day he fell in love with an elf nurse.

One fine evening, they went back to her place. She put on some soft music and led him into the bedroom.

He decided to avoid a problem and told her of his problem.

“Don’t worry,” She said, “I’m a nurse. I won’t laugh.”

The embarrassed elf drops his trousers.

“It’s OK,” she said, “I’ve seen lots smaller than that.”

“Really?” the relieved elf asked.

She nodded, “Yes, I used to work in a maternity ward.”

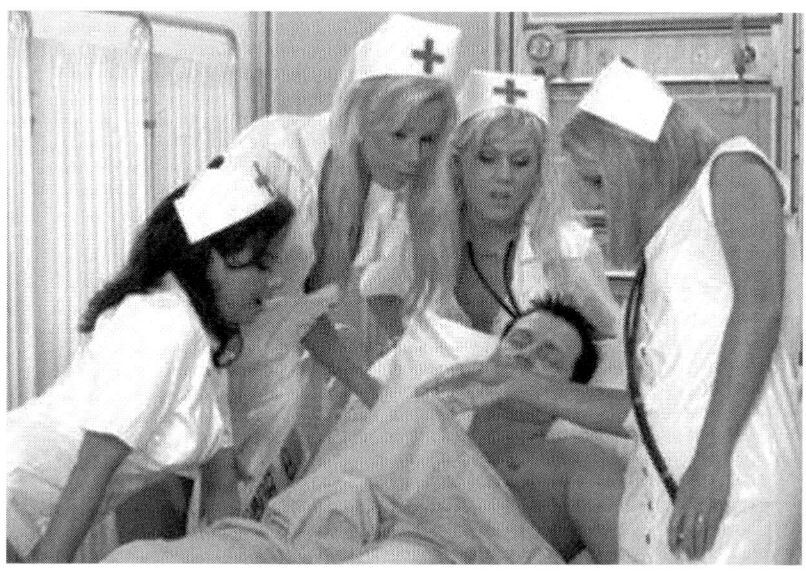

FOR AILMENTS

- Before giving a blood transfusion, find out if the blood is affirmative or negative
- To remove dust from the eye, pull the eye down over the nose
- For a nosebleed, put the nose much lower than the body until the heart stops
- For drowning, climb on top of the person and move up and down to make artificial perspiration
- For fainting, rub the person's chest or if a lady, rub her arm above the hand, or put the head between the knees of the nearest medical doctor
- For dog bite, put the dog away for several days. If he has not recovered, then kill it
- For asphyxiation, apply artificial respiration until the patient is dead
- To prevent contraception, wear a condominium
- For head cold, use an agonizer to spray the nose until it drops in the throat
- The alimentary canal is located in the northern part of Indiana
- For snakebites, bleed the wound and rape the victim in a blanket for shock.
- For fractures: To see if the limb is broken, wiggle it back and forth.
- The skeleton is what is left after the insides have been taken out and the outsides have been taken off.

EVIL PATIENT

Ray Addy was a sick old man resting in the hospital.

There was this one young nurse that just drove him crazy. Every time she came in, she would talk to him as if he was a little child. She would say in a patronizing tone of voice, "And how are we doing this morning, or are we ready for a bath, or are we hungry?"

Old Ray finally could take it no longer. He had enough of this particular nurse.

One day, Ray received breakfast, pulled the juice off the tray, and put it on his bedside stand.

He had been given a urine bottle to fill for testing. The juice that he had put aside was apple juice, so he slowly filled the urine bottle with the juice.

The nurse came in a little later and picked up the urine bottle. Looks at it and says, "My, but it seems we are a little cloudy today"

Seizing his cue, old Ray snatched the bottle out of her hand, pops off the top, and drinks it down, saying, "Well, I'll run it through again, and maybe I can filter it better this time."

The nurse fainted.

Ray just smiled.

PHYSICAL THERAPIST

A couple of women were playing golf one sunny morning. The first of the twosome teed off and watched in horror as her ball headed directly toward a foursome of men playing the next hole.

The ball hit one of the men, and he immediately clasped his hands together at his crotch, fell to the ground, and proceeded to roll around in agony.

The woman rushed down to the man and immediately began to apologize. She explained that she was a physical therapist.

"Please allow me to help. I'm a physical therapist and I know I could relieve some of your pain if you will allow me," She told him.

"No, I'll be alright. I'll be fine in a few minutes," he replies breathlessly as he remained in the fetal position still clasping his hands together at his crotch.

She persisted, and he finally allowed her to help him.

She gently took his hands away from his crotch and moved them to the side. She loosened his pants and she put her hands inside. She began to massage him.

She then asked him, "How does that feel?"

He replied, "It feels wonderful, but my thumb still hurts like heck."

NURSING SOLUTION

A man goes to visit his eighty-five-year-old grandfather in the hospital. "How are you grandpa?" he asks.

"Feeling fine," says the old man.

"What's the food like?"

"Terrific, wonderful food."

"And the nursing?"

"Just couldn't be better. These young nurses really take care of you."

"What about sleeping? Do you sleep OK?"

"No problem at all, nine hours solid every night. At ten o'clock they bring me a cup of hot chocolate and a Viagra tablet, and that's it. I go out like a light."

The grandson is puzzled and a bit alarmed by this, so rushes off to question the Charge Nurse. "What are your nurses doing," he says, "I was told you are giving an eighty-five-year-old Viagra on a daily basis. Surely that can't be true?"

"Oh, yes," replies the nurse. "Every night at ten o'clock we give him a cup of chocolate and a Viagra tablet. It works wonderfully well. The chocolate makes him sleep and the Viagra keeps him from rolling out of bed."

NUN NURSES

Ev Hines suffered a serious heart attack and had open-heart bypass surgery.

He awakened from the surgery to find himself in the care of nuns at a Catholic hospital.

As he was recovering, a nun asked him questions regarding how he was going to pay for services. He was asked if he had health insurance.

He replied, in a raspy voice, “No health insurance.”

The nun asked if he had money in the bank.

He replied, “No money in the bank.”

The nun asked, “Do you have a relative who could help you?”

He said, “I only have a spinster sister, who is a nun.”

The nun became a little perturbed and announced, “Nuns are not spinsters. Nuns are married to God.”

Ev replied, “Great, send the bill to my brother-in-law.”

BE KIND TO NURSES

A motorcycle patrolman was rushed to the hospital with an inflamed appendix.

The doctor operated and advised him that all was well. However, the patrolman kept feeling something pulling at the hairs on his chest.

He was worried that it might be a second surgery the doctors had not told him about, so he finally got up enough energy to pull his hospital gown down, so he could look at what was making him so uncomfortable.

Taped firmly across his rather hairy chest were three wide strips of adhesive tape; the kind that doesn't come off easily.

Written in large black letters was the sentence, "Get well quick and best wishes from the nurse you gave a ticket to last week."

THREE NURSES

Three nurses went to heaven, and were awaiting their turn with Saint Peter to plead their case to enter the Pearly Gates.

The first nurse said, "I worked in an Emergency Department. We tried our best to help patients, even though occasionally we did lose one. I think I deserve to go to Heaven."

Saint Peter looks at her file and admits her to Heaven.

The second nurse says, "I worked in an Operating Room. It's a very high stress environment and we do our best. Sometimes the patients are too sick and we might lose one, but overall we try very hard."

Saint Peter looks at her file and admits her to Heaven.

The third nurse says, "I was a case manager for an HMO."

Saint Peter looks at her file. He pulls out a calculator and starts punching away at it furiously, constantly going back to the nurse's file.

After a few minutes Saint Peter looks up, smiles, and says, "Congratulations. You have been admitted to Heaven. . . for five days."

TOP TEN REASONS TO BE A NURSE

1. It pays better than fast food, although the hours aren't as good

2. Fashionable shoes and sexy white uniforms

3. Needles - It's better to give than to receive

4. Reassure your patients that all bleeding stops - eventually

5. Expose yourself to rare, exotic, and exciting new diseases

6. Interesting aromas

7. Do enough charting to navigate around the world

8. Celebrate the holidays with all your friends - at work

9. Take comfort that most of your patients survive no matter what you do to them

10. Courteous and infallible doctors who always leave clear orders in perfectly legible handwriting

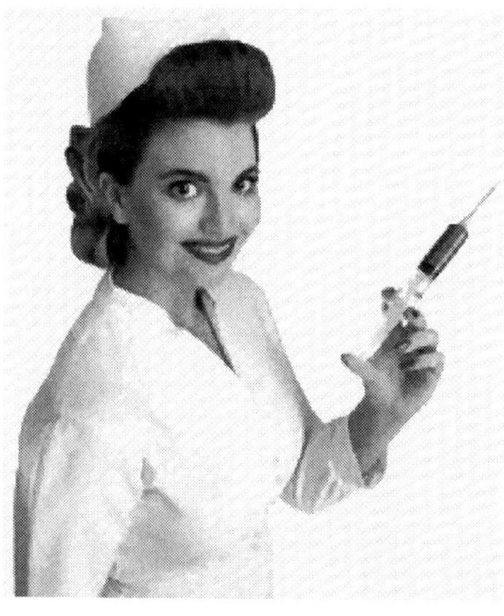

CHARACTERISTICS

A Surgeon -

Leaps short buildings in a single bound

Is as powerful as a locomotive

Is faster than a speeding bullet

Walks on water if the sea is calm

Talks with God.

An Internist -

Leaps short buildings with a running start and favorable winds

Is almost as powerful as a locomotive

Is just as fast as a speeding bullet

Walks on water in an indoor swimming pool

Talks with God, if special request is approved.

An intern -

Barely clears a pre-fabricated hut

Loses a tug of war with a locomotive

Can fire a speeding bullet

Swims well

Is occasionally addressed by God.

A Resident -

Makes high marks on a wall when trying to clear tall buildings

Is run over by a locomotive

Can sometimes handle a gun without injuring himself

Doggy paddles

Talks to animals.

An Administrator -

Runs into buildings

Recognizes locomotives two times out of three

Is not issued ammunition

Can stay afloat with a life jacket

Talks to walls.

A Nurse -

Lifts buildings and walks under them

Picks locomotives off the track

Catches speeding bullets in teeth

Freezes water with a single glance

She is God.

DOOR THREE

A physician passed away and was being screened for the destination of his soul's eternal afterlife. Unfortunately, he had been a lout, a quack, and greedy to boot, so he wasn't quite certain what to expect.

Upon arriving at the Pearly Gates, Saint Peter greeted him and informed the doctor that he would be allowed to choose from one of the doors before him, but that because of his bad attitude and misdeeds he may find the choices rather hellish.

Upon opening door number one, he witnessed fire and brimstone of truly Biblical proportions, a horrifying sight. He quickly closed it and moved on to the next.

He arrived and viewed the spectacle behind door two, and was even more horrified to observe various tortured souls ravaged by plague, disease, and other maladies to terrible to mention, while an evil guard stood watch.

With trepidation he opened door three to discover there were groups of white-coated male physicians, being waited on hand and foot by beautiful young women dressed in little more than nursing caps and white stockings.

He rushed excitedly back to Saint Peter and proclaimed, "I'll take door number three"

"Oh, no, I'm afraid that's not possible," exclaimed Saint Peter. "That's Nurses' Hell."

NEW EMPLOYEES

A hospital hired several cannibals to increase its diversity.

"You are all part of our team now," said the HR rep during the welcoming briefing. "You get all the usual benefits and you can go to the cafeteria for something to eat, but do not eat any employees."

The cannibals promised they would not eat any employees.

Four weeks later the Chief Operating Officer greeted the group and remarked, "You are all working very hard and I am pleased with your work. We have noticed a marked increase in the hospitals performance metrics. However, one of our nurses has recently disappeared. Do any of you know what might have happened to her?"

The cannibals all responded in the negative.

After the COO had left, the chief of the cannibals said to the others, "Which one of you idiots ate the nurse?"

In the back of the room, a hand rose slowly and hesitantly.

"You fool!" the leader raged. "For four weeks we have been eating managers and doctors and no one noticed anything, but now you had to ruin it by eating someone who actually does something."

REASONS TO DATE A NURSE

- ☞ They assess all areas of the body
- ☞ Scrubs make for easy access
- ☞ They are clean
- ☞ They don't gag
- ☞ They know your body inside and out
- ☞ They know mouth to mouth
- ☞ Two words. . . Sponge Bath
- ☞ They know how to penetrate things
- ☞ They always have a rubber on hand
- ☞ They can go all night long
- ☞ They are used to handling all types of bodily fluids
- ☞ They know all the right places to palpate
- ☞ They know how to properly apply restraints
- ☞ They know lots of different positions
- ☞ They know lubrication is helpful in any procedure
- ☞ They are always up for a good game of doctor

Pharmacy

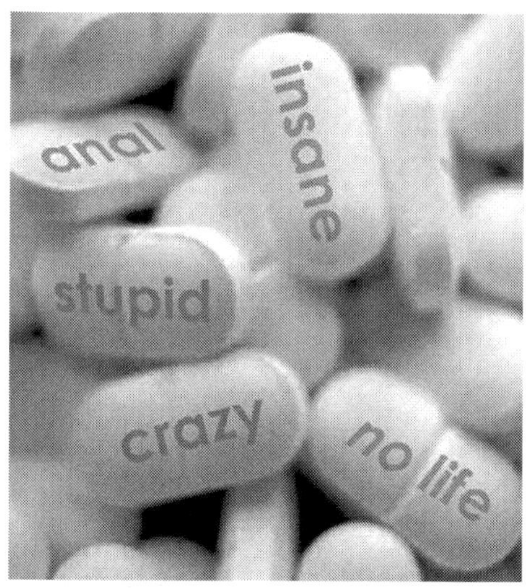

SMALL DOSES

All drugs have a generic name. Tylenol is Acetaminophen, Advil is Ibuprofen, etc. For the last few months, the FDA has been looking for a generic name for Viagra.

Yesterday they announced they have finally settled on Mycoxafailin.

Pfizer is making the announcement today that Viagra will soon be available in liquid form, and will be marketed by Pepsi Cola as a power beverage suitable for use as-is or as a mixer, under the name "Mount and Do."

Pepsi's proposed ad campaign suggests, "It will now be possible for a man to literally pour himself a stiff one."

≈ ≈ ≈

"Advice for the day: If you have a lot of tension and you get a headache, do what it says on the aspirin bottle.
Take two aspirin and keep away from children.

In the 60's people took acid to make the world weird. Now the world is so weird, people take prozac to make it normal.

≈ ≈ ≈

A lady walks into the drug store and asks for some arsenic.

The pharmacist asks, "Madam, what do you want with arsenic?"

The lady says, "To kill my husband."

"I can't sell you any for that reason," he says.

The lady reaches into her purse and pulls out a photo of a man and a woman in a compromising position. The man is her husband and the lady is the pharmacist's wife.

He looks at the photo and says, "Oh, I didn't know you had a prescription."

News Flash October - All physicians contracted to Kaiser Healthcare have gone out on strike.

Kaiser officials say that they will have a statement for the press as soon as they can get a pharmacist out there to read the physicians' picket signs.

I guess we could reduce the Viagra prescription

Pfizer Corp. is making the announcement today that VIAGRA will soon be available in liquid form and will be marketed by Pepsi Cola as a power beverage suitable for use 'as is', or a mixer. Pepsi's proposed ad campaign claims, "It will now be possible for a man to literally pour himself a stiff one." Obviously they can no longer call this a soft drink. This additive gives new meaning to the names of cocktails, highballs, and just a good old fashion stiff drink. Pepsi will market the new concoction by the name of 'Mount and Do'.

A bartender is just a pharmacist with a limited inventory.

Marcia walks into a drug store and says she wants to buy a condom for her boyfriend. The druggist says, “Fine. That’ll be a dollar ten.”
“A dollar ten?” she asks.
“Yes,” the druggist says. “One dollar for the condom and ten cents for the tax.”
“Tacks?” says Marcia, “I thought you rolled them on.”

John Mascitti went into a drug store and asked for some liniment. “Walk this way” said the clerk. John said, “If I could walk that way, I wouldn’t need the liniment.”

There was a family gathering, with all generations around the table. Mischievous teenagers put a Viagra tablet into Grandpa’s drink and after a while, Grandpa excused himself because he had to go to the bathroom. When he returned, his trousers were soaking wet all over.

“What happened, Grandpa?” he was asked by his concerned grandchildren.

He answered, “I don’t really know. I had to go to the bathroom, so I took it out and started to pee, but then I saw that it wasn’t mine, so I put it back.”

~~~ ~~~ ~~~

~~~ ~~~ ~~~

A lady walked into a pharmacy and spoke to the pharmacist.

She asked, "Do you have Viagra?"

"Yes," he answered.

She asked, "Does it work?"

"Yes."

"Can you get it over the counter?"

"I can if I take two," he replied proudly.

~~~ ~~~ ~~~

Yucky Chucky's parents took him to the doctor. They explained that although their little angel appeared to be in good health, they were concerned about his rather small penis.

After examining Chucky, the doctor confidently declared, "Just feed him pancakes. That should solve the problem."

The next morning when Chucky arrived at breakfast, there was a large stack of warm pancakes in the middle of the table.

Gee, mom," Chucky asked, "Are all of these for me?"

"Just take two," she replied. "The rest are for your father."
~~~

≈ ≈ ≈

A duck went into a drugstore to buy some condoms.
The druggist said, "You want me to put that on your bill?"
The duck said, "Just what kind of a duck do you think I am?"

≈ ≈ ≈

A woman walks into a drugstore and asks the pharmacist if he sells extra large condoms.
He replies, "Yes we do. Would you like to buy some?"
She responds, "No sir, but do you mind if I wait around here until someone does?"

≈ ≈ ≈

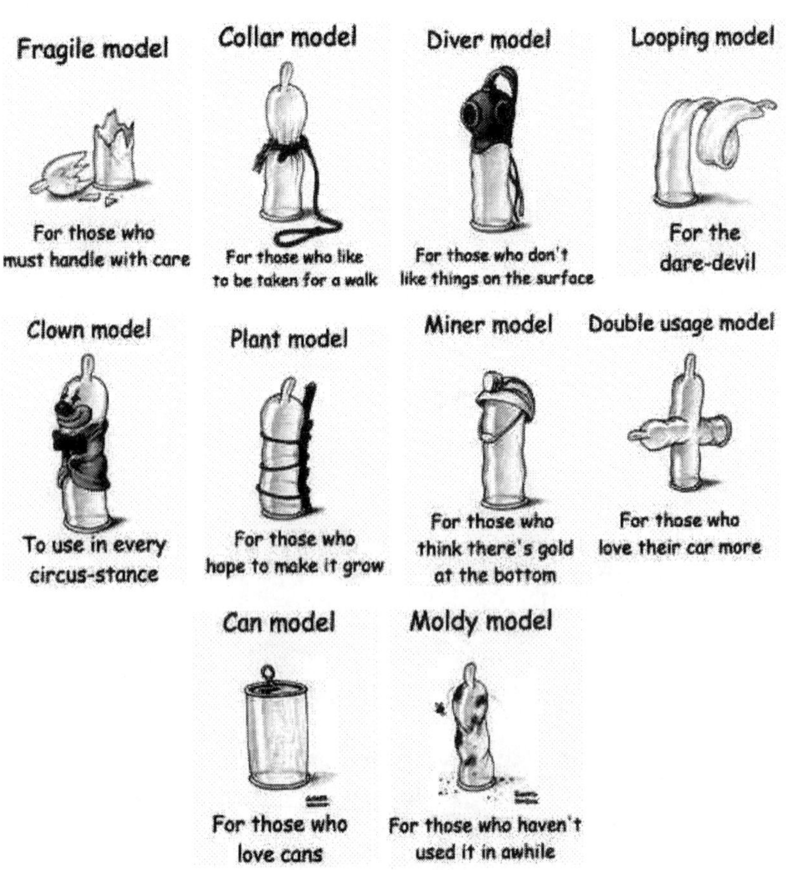

More new condom models

♒ ♒ ♒

Condoms should be used on every conceivable occasion

♒ ♒ ♒

A woman walked into the pharmacy and asked for a vibrator. The pharmacist gestured with his index finger and said, “Come this way.”

She said, “If I could come that way, I wouldn’t need a vibrator.”

♒ ♒ ♒

The makers of Viagra are announcing that they have developed a pill to increase vaginal wetness in females. The new pill will be called Niagra.

♒ ♒ ♒

Older folks have discovered a new combination, Viagra and Doan’s Pills.
The back won’t peter out and the peter won’t back out.

♒ ♒ ♒

After receiving his medication from the pharmacist, the customer asks, “Are these time release pills?” The pharmacist replies, “Yes. They begin to work after your check clears.”

♒ ♒ ♒

Calling an illegal alien an ‘undocumented immigrant’ is like calling a drug dealer an ‘unlicensed pharmacist’.

♒ ♒ ♒

A doctor is scheduled to give a speech at the local AMA dinner. He jots down notes for his speech.

Unfortunately, when he stands in front of his colleagues later that night, he finds that he can’t read his notes, so he asks, “Is there a pharmacist in the house?”

♒ ♒ ♒

PILLS

A row of bottles on my shelf
caused me to analyze myself.

One yellow pill I have to pop
goes to my heart so it won't stop.

A little white one that I take
goes to my hands so they won't shake

The blue ones that I use a lot
tell me I'm happy when I'm not

The purple pill goes to my brain
and tells me that I have no pain.

The capsules tell me not to wheeze
or cough or choke or even sneeze.

The red ones, smallest of them all
go to my blood so I won't fall.

The orange ones, very big and bright
prevent my leg cramps in the night.

Such an array of brilliant pills
helping to cure all of my ills.

But what I'd really like to know
is what tells each one just where to go.

PHARMACIST FATHER

A girl asks her boyfriend to come over Friday night and have dinner with her parents. Since this is such a big event, the girl announces to her boyfriend that after dinner, she would like to go out and make love for the first time.

Well, the boy is ecstatic, but he has never had sex before, so he takes a trip to the pharmacist to get some condoms. The pharmacist helps the boy for about an hour. He tells the boy everything there is to know about condoms and sex.

At the register, the pharmacist asks the boy how many condoms he'd like to buy, a three-pack, ten-pack, or family pack. The boy insists on the family pack because he thinks he will be rather busy, because it is his first time.

That night, the boy shows up at the girl's parent's house and meets his girlfriend at the door. "Oh, I'm so excited for you to meet my parents, come on in."

The boy goes inside and is taken to the dinner table where the girl's parents are seated. The boy quickly offers to say grace and bows his head.

A minute passes, and the boy is still deep in prayer, with his head down. Ten minutes pass, and still no movement from the boy. Finally, after twenty minutes with his head down, the girlfriend leans over and whispers to the boyfriend, "I had no idea you were this religious."

The boy turns, and whispers back, "I had no idea your father was a pharmacist."

ON TEENAGERS, ADULT:

Statistics show that teen pregnancy drops off significantly after age 25.

Mary Anne Tebedo, Republican state senator from Colorado Springs (contributed by Harry F. Pancoe)

DEODORANT

A blonde walks into a pharmacy and asks for some rectum deodorant. The pharmacist explains to the woman they don't sell rectum deodorant, and never have.

Unfazed, the blonde assures the pharmacist that she has been buying the stuff from drug stores on a regular basis and would like some more.

"I'm sorry," says the pharmacist. "We don't have any."

"But I always buy it at drug stores," says the blonde.

"Do you have the container that it came in?" asks the pharmacist.

"Yes," said the blonde. "I'll go home and get it."

She returns with the container and hands it to the pharmacist who looks at it and says to her, "This is just a normal stick of underarm deodorant"

The blonde snatches the container back and reads out loud from the container,

"To apply, push up bottom."

TEQUILA CURE

Do you have feelings of inadequacy? Do you suffer from shyness? Do you sometimes wish you were more assertive?

If you answered yes to any of these questions, ask your doctor or pharmacist about Tequila.

Tequila is the safe, natural way to feel better and more confident about yourself and your actions. Tequila can help ease you out of your shyness and let you tell the world that you're ready and willing to do just about anything.

You will notice the benefits of Tequila almost immediately, and with a regimen of regular doses you can overcome any obstacles that prevent you from living the life you want to live. Shyness and awkwardness will be a thing of the past, and you will discover many talents you never knew you had.

Stop hiding and start living, with Tequila.

Tequila may not be right for everyone. Women who are pregnant or nursing should not use Tequila. However, women who wouldn't mind nursing or becoming pregnant are encouraged to try it.

Side effects may include: dizziness, nausea, vomiting, incarceration, erotic lustfulness, loss of motor control, loss of clothing, loss of money, loss of virginity, delusions of grandeur, table dancing, headache, dehydration, dry mouth, and a desire to sing Karaoke and play all-night rounds of Strip Poker, Truth or Dare, and Naked Twister.

HERBAL PRESCRIPTION

Brady McCoy has been feeling really bad for about three weeks so he goes to see his doctor.

The doctor says, "Look, I don't know what you have, but it could be serious, so why don't you go and visit this specialist I know."

So Brady went to the specialist and the specialist said, "You have this rare sickness, only one person every ten years is afflicted with it. The only cure is made in Australia in a little town called Mercy, about four hundred miles from Sidney. By the way, you have one week to live."

He went home, packed his bags, and caught the first flight he could to Sidney. When he arrived, he rented a car and drove to Mercy, Australia. When arrived, he found it was a town with a population of one.

Brady walked up to the only house in the village and an old doctor answered.

"You have to help me," he said, "I'm dying of this rare illness, and I have only four days to live."

The old doctor invited him in. "I must give you my special Koala Bear Tea. It is the only thing that will cure you."

The doctor went out to get the supplies, one koala, a few birds, and such, and he boiled them together and gave them to the man with bones and feathers and dirt sticking up.

Mister McCoy looked at it repulsed and asked if it could be strained. The old doctor looked horrified and said, "Oh no. *The Koala Tea of Mercy is never strained.*"

HAIR REMOVER

A lady found out her dog could hardly hear so she took it to the veterinarian. He found the problem was hair in its ears and cleaned both ears and the dog could hear fine.

The vet told the lady if she wanted to keep this from reoccurring, she should go to the store and get some Nair hair remover and rub its ears once a month.

The lady goes to the drug store and gets some "Nair" hair remover. At the register, the druggist tells her, "If you're going to use this under your arms, don't use deodorant for a few days."

The lady says, "I'm not using it under my arms."

The druggist says, "If you're using it on your legs, don't use lotion for a couple days."

The lady says, "I'm not using it on my legs either, and, if you must know, I'm using it on my schnauzer."

The druggist says, "Stay off your bicycle for a week."

DRUGS FOR WOMEN

ANTIBOYOTICS: When administered to teenage girls, is highly effective in improving grades, freeing up phone lines, and reducing money spent on makeup.

ANTI-TALKSIDENTA: Spray carried in a purse or wallet to be used on anyone too eager to share their life stories with total strangers in elevators.

BUYAGRA: Injectable stimulant taken prior to shopping. Increases potency, duration, and credit limit of spending spree.

DAMNITOL: Take two and the rest of the world can go to hell for up to eight full hours.

DUMBEROL: When taken with Peptobimbo, can cause dangerously low IQ, resulting in enjoyment of country music and pickup trucks.

EMPTYNESTROGEN: Suppository that eliminates melancholy and loneliness by reminding you of how awful they were as teenagers and how you couldn't wait till they moved out.

FLIPITOR: Increases life expectancy of commuters by controlling road rage and the urge to flip off other drivers.

JACKASSPIRIN: Relieves headache caused by a man who can't remember your birthday, anniversary, phone number, or to lift the toilet seat.

MENICILLIN: Potent anti-boy-otic for older women. Increases resistance to such lethal lines as, "You make me want to be a better person."

PEPTOBIMBO: Liquid silicone drink for single women. Two full cups swallowed before an evening out increases breast size, decreases intelligence, and prevents conception.

ST. MOMMA'S WORT: Plant extract that treats mom's depression by rendering preschoolers unconscious for up to two days.

PRESCRIPTIONS

John is ninety-two and Marge is ninety-one. They are all excited about their decision to get married. They go for a stroll to discuss the wedding and on their way pass a drugstore.

John suggests that they go in. He addresses the man behind the counter and says, "Are you the owner?"

The pharmacist answers, "Yes."

John: "Do you sell heart medication?"

Pharmacist: "Of course we do."

John: "How about medicine for circulation?"

Pharmacist: "All kinds."

John: "Medicine for rheumatism?"

Pharmacist: "Definitely."

John: "How about Viagra?"

Pharmacist: "Of course."

John: "Medicine for memory?"

Pharmacist: "Yes, a large variety."

John: "What about vitamins and sleeping pills?"

Pharmacist: "Absolutely."

John turns to Marge: "Sweetheart, we might as well register our wedding gift list with them."

THE TEST

Jack says to Paul, “My elbow hurts like hell. I need to see a doctor.”

“You don’t have to spend that kind of money,” Paul replies. “Amy found a diagnostic computer down at the Wal-Mart pharmacy. Just give it a urine sample and the computer will tell you what’s wrong and what to do about it. It takes ten seconds and costs ten dollars, a lot cheaper than a doctor.”

Jack goes back to his car and deposits a urine sample in a small jar and takes it to the Wal-Mart pharmacy. He deposits ten dollars and the computer lights up and asks for the urine sample. He pours the sample into the slot and waits. Ten seconds later the computer ejects a printout, “You have tennis elbow. Soak your arm in warm water and avoid heavy activity. It will improve in two weeks.

That evening while thinking how amazing this new technology was, Jack began wondering if the computer could be fooled.

He mixed some tap water, a stool sample from his dog, urine samples from his wife and daughter, and a sperm sample for good measure.

He hurries back to the pharmacy to check the results. He deposits ten dollars, pours in his concoction, and awaits the results.

The computer prints the following:

Your tap water is too hard. Get a water softener on aisle nine.

Your dog has ringworm. Get anti-fungal shampoo on aisle seven.

Your daughter has a cocaine habit. Get her into rehab.

Your wife is pregnant with twins. They aren’t yours. Get a lawyer.

If you don’t stop playing with yourself, your elbow will never get better.

CANDY

One day on the way home from work, Bill Biermann stopped at the local pharmacy and while Bill was checking out, he picked up some candy to take home for him and his 7-year old son. It was a bag of gold foil covered chocolate candy coins.

There were many sizes, from dimes to dollars. Bill took the bag home and the two of them opened the bag and ate all of the coins. His son took the bigger dollar-sized ones and Bill took the smaller ones.

The next day, his wife and son and he stopped at the pharmacy again to pick up a few things. While Bill and his wife were shopping, they noticed their son had picked up a gold coin condom.

Before they could catch him, he took it up to the counter and asked the pharmacist, “What’s this?”

The woman looked very serious and said, “That’s a condom, son.”

To which Bill’s son replied, “My dad bought me some of these yesterday.”

With a disgusted look on her face, the pharmacist replied, “Those are not for children, young man.”

To this Bill’s son replied, “Then I’ll buy this one for my dad. He likes the little ones.”

HEALING ELIXIR

Millions of Americans are overweight. Obesity is one of the most dangerous and unattractive medical crises facing our nation. Everyone has tried all the latest pills, diets, and massage treatments. There is always the option of regular exercise and a moderate diet, but not many have the time or energy.

Now you don't have to restrict your favorite foods. You don't even have to exercise. Go ahead and eat that second piece of cheesecake. With our plan, you can still attain any weight you choose.

It is guaranteed to help you loose five, ten, twenty pounds - you decide.

Best of all, it's from nature, so you know it's safe. Unlike artificial, sterile pharmaceutical factories, nature is in perfect balance. All living things from nature are beneficial for your health.

Here's how it works. We collect crystal clear water from a natural unadulterated river. We wish you could see the source with tall sycamore trees swaying in the breeze.

Just upstream, a family of industrious beavers has built a series of impressive dams. The industry of the beavers imparts a special essence to the waters. These beaver and other of nature's essences cleanse your system in a profound way that you have never experienced.

A day or two after you drink our healing water; you will begin to notice your body cleansing itself. The weight just flows away. Once you have lost as much weight as you want, it is easy to stop.

Just page your family doctor. He or she should be available day or night, and ask him to call in a prescription for Kaopectate. After one or two doses, the cleansing process slows down, and your weight will stabilize. That's all there is to it.

Keep a few extra bottles of our nature's own river elixir on hand if those troublesome pounds start to come back. The longer it sits, the better it works.

NEW PILLS

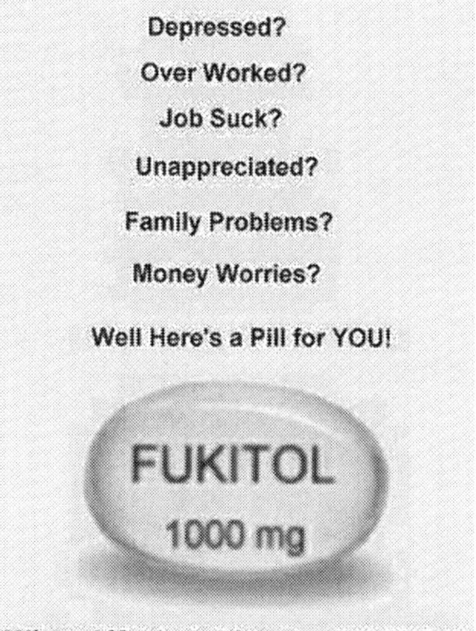

Suffering from ED (Excessive Dishonesty)

Can't remember the truth?

Worn down by getting caught in lies?

Spending too much time dreaming up new stories?

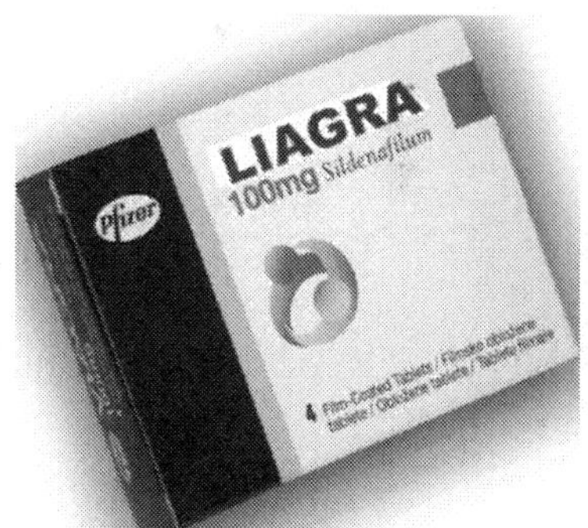

Try LIAGRA

- -- **Stronger, longer lasting fabrications**
- -- **Tell lies faster, with more energy**
- -- **Remove all sense of remorse**
- -- **Believe your own stories**

Warnings:

- Do not use this product if you still have a conscience
- The speed of lies may exceed lung capacity so contact your physician if you feel short of breath.
- Loss of vision (philosophically speaking) may occur.
- Expect some loss of hearing...criticism
- To reverse effects, contact an Exorcist

- I was shot at by snipers
- I was for/against NAFTA
- Illegals should/shouldn't be given a drivers license
- I didn't know Bill was a cheater
- Chelsea was jogging around the Trade Center on Sept. 11, 2001
- White Water?
- Travelgate?
- What Pardons?

MOTION SICKNESS

Walt Meiers had been retired for years when his wife of forty years suggested, "Why don't we take a cruise for a week and make wild passionate love like we did when we were young?"

He thought it over and agreed. He put on his hat and coat and went down to Agemy's corner store. He stepped up to the counter and asked for a bottle of seasick pills and a box of condoms.

Upon returning home his wife, Joanne greeted him at the door saying, "You know dear, I've been thinking it over and I see no reason why we couldn't manage a month long cruise so we could relax and make wild passionate love like we did when we were young."

He smiled, turned around, and went back to the pharmacy. He stepped up and ordered twelve bottles of seasick pills and a dozen boxes of condoms.

Upon returning back home Joanne met him on the porch with a big smile on her face.

"Walt, I have a marvelous idea. You know, now that our children are all on their own, there's nothing to stop us from cruising around the world."

"I'll be right back," he said. Back to the drug store he went. When he approached the pharmacy counter the druggist looked up with a puzzled grin.

Walt sheepishly ordered two hundred bottles of seasick pills and the same number of boxes of condoms.

The pharmacist busied himself filling the order then passed the wrapped package across the counter saying, "You know, Walt, you've been doing business with me for over thirty years. I certainly don't mean to pry, but if it makes you that sick, why do you do it so much?"

VIAGRA

Dad and mom were living with their son and daughter-in-law. Dad noticed that his son had a bottle of Viagra and asked if he could have one.

His son said, "Dad, I don't think you should take one. They're very strong and very expensive."

"I know, but I want to try one. How much are they?"

His son said, "They are ten dollars each."

The father only had a fifty dollar bill, but was going to the bank and said he would leave ten dollars under his son's pillow that night.

The next morning his son found a hundred and ten dollars under his pillow. He went to his father and said, "Dad, I told you it was only ten dollars and there was a hundred and ten dollars under my pillow."

The father said, "I put the ten dollars there as we agreed, the extra hundred is a tip from your mother."

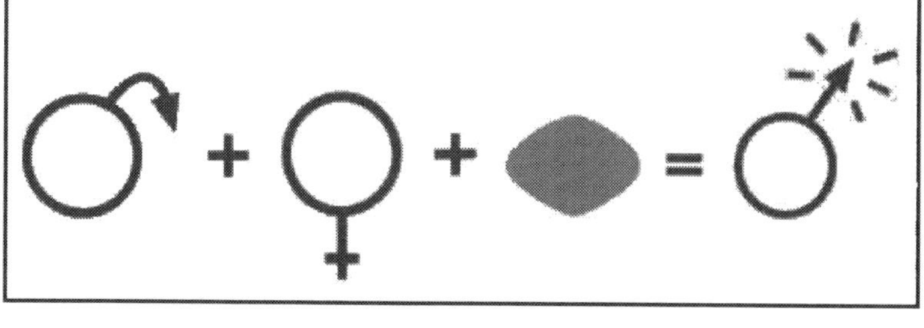

SEVERE PROBLEM

Richard Wall walks into a pharmacy and goes to the counter. Standing behind the counter is a young woman.

“May I speak to the pharmacist?” he asks.

She replies, “I am the pharmacist.”

Richard looks very uncomfortable, and asks for a male pharmacist, as he has a male problem.

She informs him that only she and her sister work at this particular pharmacy, but not to worry as they have heard everything before.

He blushes and says, “Well, I really do need help, so I guess I’ll ask you. I have a problem. I have a constant erection, and nothing I do seems to get rid of it. It’s been like this for two weeks. Can you give me anything for it?”

The woman looks thoughtful, and says, “Hold on, I’ll go in back and ask my sister.”

After a couple of minutes she returns and says, “We will give you half of the business and its profits, but that’s all we can give you for it.”

INSULTING PHARMACIST

Jonathon Overton arrived home and was met at the door by his sobbing wife. Tearfully she explained, "The pharmacist insulted me terribly this morning on the phone."

Immediately, Jonathon went to confront the druggist and demand an apology. Before he could say more than a word or two, the druggist told him, "Hold it. You must listen to my side of the story.

This morning the alarm failed to go off, so I was late getting up. I went without breakfast and hurried out to the car, only to realize that I locked the house with both house and car keys inside."

I had to break a window to get my keys. Then I drove a bit too fast and got a speeding ticket. When I was about three blocks from the store, I got a flat tire. After I fixed it and finally got to the pharmacy, there was a bunch of people waiting for me to open up. I got the store opened and started waiting on these people and the phone was ringing the whole time.

Then I had to break a roll of quarters against the cash register drawer to make change and they spilled all over the floor. I got down on my hands and knees to pick them up and the phone rang again. When I came up to answer it, I cracked my head on the open cash drawer, which made me stagger back against a showcase with a bunch of perfume bottles on it and they all hit the floor and broke.

Meanwhile, the phone is still ringing, and I finally got to answer it. It was your wife. She wanted to know how to use a rectal thermometer. Believe me Mister Overton, all I did was tell her."

NEW PILLS FOR MEN

BUYAGRA - Married and otherwise attached men reported a sudden urge to buy their sweeties expensive jewelry and gifts after taking this drug for only two days. Still to be seen: whether the drug can be continued for a period longer than your favorite store's return limit.

CAPAGRA - Caused test subjects to become uncharacteristically fastidious about lowering toilet seats and replacing toothpaste caps. Subjects on higher doses were seen dusting furniture.

CHILDAGRA - Men taking this drug reported a sudden, overwhelming urge to perform more child-care tasks - especially cleaning up spills and little accidents.

COMPLIMENTRA - In clinical trials, 82 percent of middle-aged men administered this drug noticed that their wives had a new hairstyle. Currently being tested to see if its effects extend to noticing new clothing.

DIRECTRA - A dose of this drug given to men before leaving on car trips caused 72 percent of them to stop and ask for directions when they got lost, compared to a control group where only 0.2 percent asked for directions.

LYAGRA - This drug causes men to be less than truthful when they are asked about their sexual affairs. Will be available in Regular, Grand Jury and Presidential Strength versions.

NEGA-SPORTAGRA - This drug had the strange effect of making men want to turn off televised sports and actually converse with other family members.

NEGA-VIAGRA - Has the exact opposite effect of Viagra. Currently undergoing clinical trials on sitting U.S. presidents.

PRYAGRA - About to fail its clinical trial, this drug gave men in the test group an irresistible urge to dig into the personal affairs of other people. Note: Apparent overdose turned three test subjects into special prosecutors.

STOMACH ACHE

A bear walks into a bar and goes up to the bartender, "Give me a beer, or I will eat one or your patrons."

The bartender refuses so the bear picks up a customer at random and chows him down.

He once again approaches the bar and says, "Give me a beer or I will eat one of your patrons."

Once again the bartender refuses. The bear looks around, grabs a beautiful blonde nearby, gobbles her down, and then proceeds to grab his stomach, and fall into a deep coma.

Several hours later, the bear awakens, gets up, and stumbles back to the bar. "What happened?" he growls.

The bartender answers, "That was a '*bar bitch you ate'*."

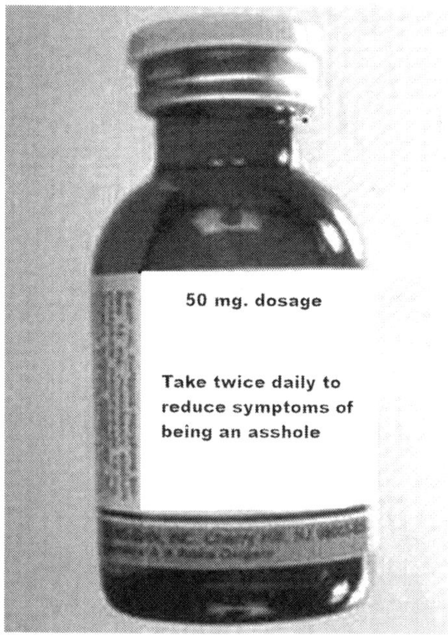

EXPERIMENTAL PILLS

Doc, you have to help me. My wife just isn't interested in sex anymore. Don't you have a pill or something I can give her?"

"I can't prescribe. . ."

"Doc, we've been friends for years. Have you ever seen me this upset? I am desperate! I can't think, I can't concentrate, and my life is going utterly to hell. You have to help me."

The doctor opens his desk drawer and removes a small bottle of pills. "Ordinarily, I wouldn't do this. These are experimental; the tests so far indicate that they're very powerful. Don't give her more than one, just one."

"I don't know doc, she's awfully cold."

"One. No more. Put it in her coffee."

"OK."

The guy expresses gratitude and leaves for home, where his wife has dinner waiting. When dinner is finished, she goes to the kitchen to bring dessert.

The man hastily pulls the pills from his pocket and drops one into his wife's coffee. He reflects for a moment, hesitates, and then drops in a second pill.

Then he begins to worry. The doctor did say they were powerful.

Then inspiration strikes, so he drops one pill into his own coffee.

His wife returns with the shortcake and they enjoy their dessert and coffee. Sure enough, a few minutes after they finish, his wife shudders a little, sighs deeply and heavily, and a strange look comes over her. In a near-whisper and a tone of voice he has never heard her use before, she says, "I need a man."

His eyes glitter and his hands tremble as he replies, "Me too."

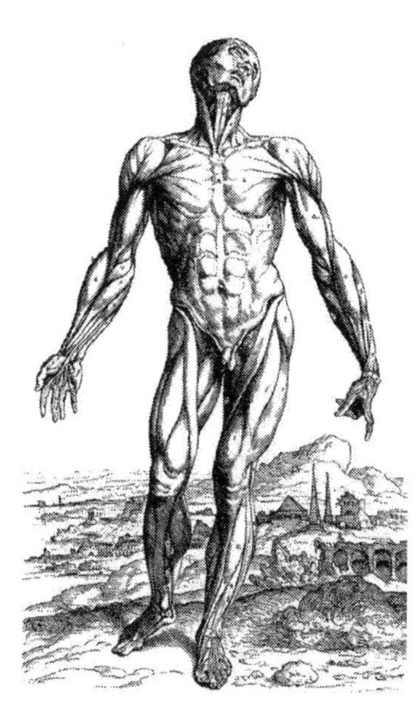

SYNAPSES

A guy walks into the psychiatrist wearing only shorts made from plastic wrap.

The psychiatrist says, “Well, I can clearly see your nuts.”

🚹 🚺

A blonde had something wrong with her brain so she went to see a doctor. After the medical examination, the doctor told her, “Your brain has two parts, one is left, and the other is right. Your left brain has nothing right. Your right brain has nothing left.”

🚹 🚺

Doctor, doctor, I’ve lost my memory.
When did it happen?
When did what happen?

🚹 🚺

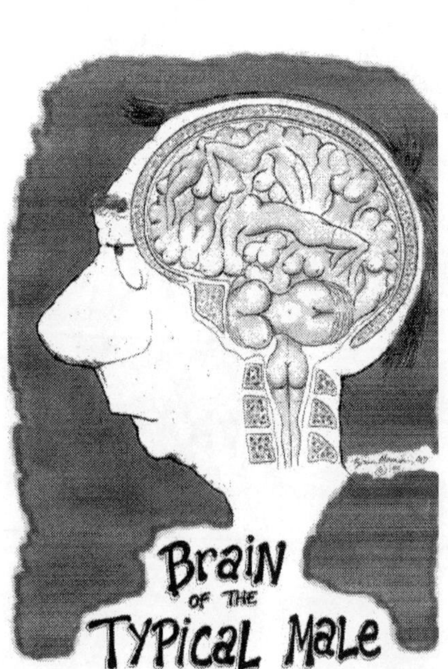

The human brain is like a freight car – guaranteed to have a certain capacity, but sometimes running empty.

Two psychiatrists were at a convention. As they conversed over a drink, one asked, “What was your most difficult case?”

The other replied, “I had a patient who lived in a pure fantasy world. He believed that an uncle in South America was going to die and leave him a fortune. All day long he waited for a letter to arrive from an attorney. He never went out, he never did anything, he merely sat around and waited for this fantasy letter from this fantasy uncle. I worked with this man eight years.”

“What was the result?”

“It was an eight year struggle. Every day for eight years, but I finally cured him. . . and then that stupid letter arrived.”

An absent-minded man went to see a psychiatrist.
“My trouble is that I keep forgetting things.”
“How long has this been going on?” asked the psychiatrist.
“How long has what been going on?” said the man.

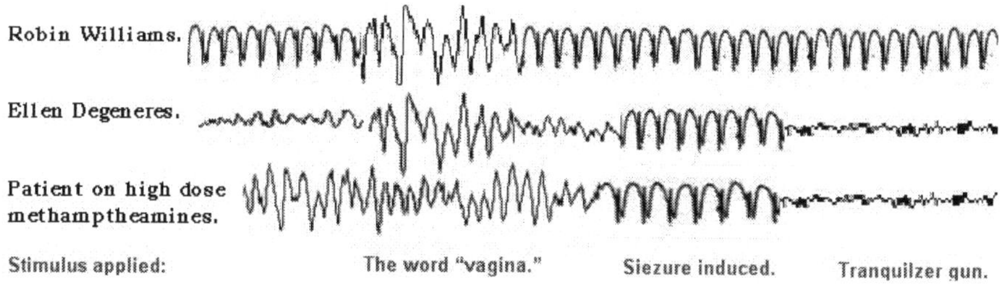

Everyone has a photographic memory
Some just don’t have any film.

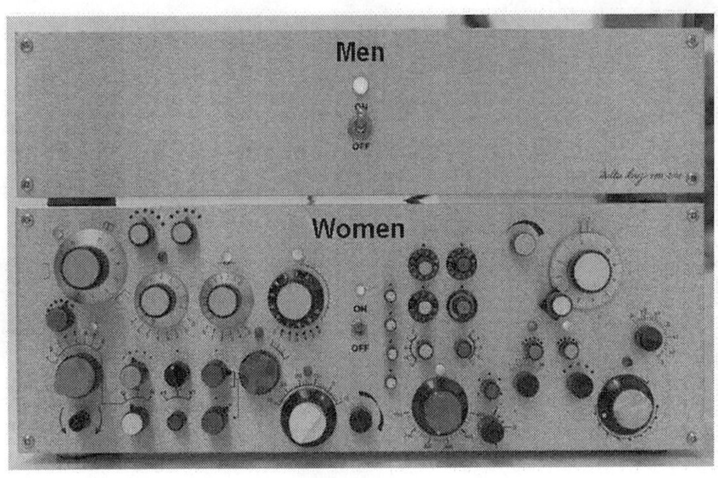

How many psychoanalysts does it take to change a light bulb?
How many do you think?

'A frog in my throat' means hoarse from a cold. The saying originated in the Middle Ages, when infections were sometimes treated by putting a live frog head first into the patient's mouth. By inhaling, the frog was believed to draw the patient's infection into its own body.

A woman went to her doctor and complained that her husband was 300% impotent.

The doctor replied, "I'm not sure I understand what you mean."

She answered, "Well, the first 100% you can imagine. In addition, he burned his tongue and broke his finger!"

Humans are more intelligent than beasts because human brains have more convulsions.

A man was walking down the street past a Mental Institution which had a ten foot wooden fence surrounding it. He heard a number of people shouting "13 . . . 13 . . . 13" and he became curious.

He found a knothole big enough to look through, bent over, and peered in. He was immediately poked in the eye by a finger as a new chant went up . . ."14 . . . 14 . . . 14."

"Doctor, doctor, I keep thinking I'm a goat"
"How long have you had this problem?"
"Ever since I was a kid."

Three aspiring psychiatrists from various colleges were attending their first class on emotional extremes.

"Just to establish some parameters," said the professor to the student from the University of Texas, "What is the opposite of joy?"

"Sadness," said the student.

"And the opposite of depression?" he asked of the young lady from Harvard.

"Elation," she answered.

"And you sir," he said to the young man from Texas A&M. "How about the opposite of woe?"

The Aggie replied, "I believe that would be giddy-up."

Is it common for seventy year olds to have problems with short term memory storage?

Storing memory is not a problem, retrieving it is a problem.

Back away and look again

Neurotics build castles in the sky.
Psychotics live in them.
Psychiatrists collect the rent.

"Doctor, I keep thinking I'm a pair of curtains"
"Pull yourself together man."

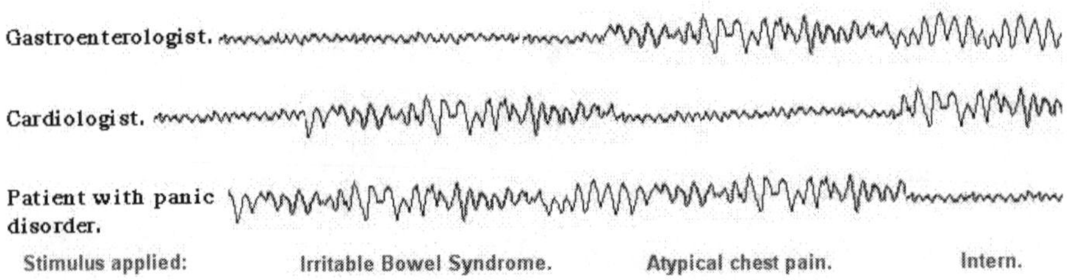

Gastroenterologist.

Cardiologist.

Patient with panic disorder.

Stimulus applied: Irritable Bowel Syndrome. Atypical chest pain. Intern.

Your heart pumps about 2,000 gallons of blood each day.

Having 'a screw loose' means something is wrong with a person. The origins of this saying, dates back to the 1700s and the cotton industry, when the industrial revolution made mass production of textiles possible for the first time. Huge mills sprang up to take advantage of the new technology, but it was difficult to keep all the machines running properly; any machine that broke down or produced defective cloth was said to have 'a screw loose'.

What's the difference between a psychologist and a magician?
A psychologist pulls habits out of rats.

After stopping for drinks at an illegal bar, a Zimbabwean bus driver found that the twenty mental patients he was supposed to be transporting from Harare to Bulawayo had escaped. Not wanting to admit his incompetence, the driver went to a nearby bus stop and offered everyone waiting there a free ride. He then delivered the passengers to the mental hospital, telling the staff that the patients were very excitable and prone to bizarre fantasies. The deception wasn't discovered for three days.

It has recently been discovered that research causes cancer in rats.

Be an organ donor – unbuckle.

Sexual survival depends on knowing the difference between a birthmark and a rash.

🚹 🚺

A psychiatrist was conducting a group therapy session with four young mothers and their small children.

"You all have obsessions," he observed.

He looked at the first mother and said, "You are obsessed with eating. In fact, you even named your daughter Candy."

He turned to the second mom and said, "Your obsession is with money and it manifests itself in your child's name, Penny."

He then turned to the third mom and said, "Your obsession is alcohol. This too shows itself in your child's name, Brandy."

At this point, the fourth mother quietly got up, took her little boy by the hand, and whispered, "Come on Dick, we're leaving."

🚹 🚺

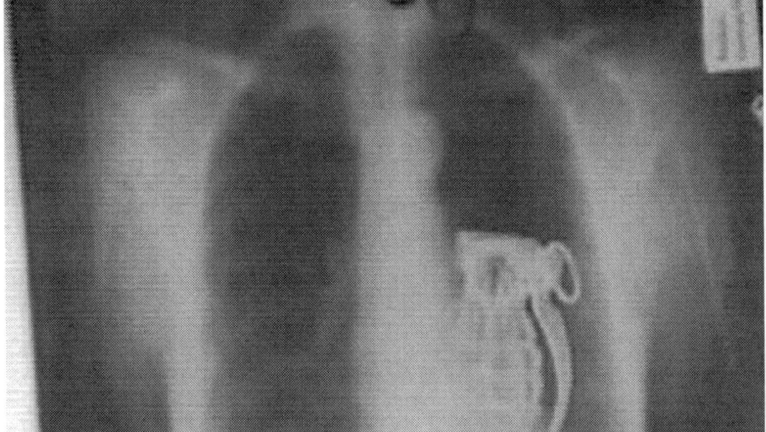

Muslim X-ray

A medical student received a failing grade in Radiology. He approached the professor and demanded to know the reason.

"Do you remember the self X-ray you took?" asked the professor.

"I do," said the student.

"A fine picture of your lungs, stomach, and liver."

"If it's a fine picture, why did you give me an F?" asked the student.

"I had no choice," said the professor. "You didn't put your heart in it."

A man decided to paint the toilet while his wife was away. His wife came home sooner than he expected, used the toilet, and got the seat stuck to her rear.

She was understandably distraught about this and asked her husband to drive her to the doctor. She put a large overcoat on to cover the seat before they went.

When they got to the doctor's office, the man lifted his wife's coat to show him their predicament. The man asked, "Doctor, have you ever seen anything like this before?"

"Well, yes," the doctor replied, "But never framed."

A few days before his proctologic exam, a one-eyed man accidentally swallowed his glass eye. He was worried for a while, but there were no ill effects, so he forgot about it.

Once he was in the doctor's office, the man followed his instructions, undressed and bent over. The first thing the proctologist saw when he looked up the man's butt was that glass eye staring right back at him.

"Mister Jones," said the doctor, "You really have to learn to trust me."

BODY PARTS

When the body was first made, all of the parts wanted to be boss.

The brain said, "Since I control everything, and I do all of the thinking, I should be boss."

The feet said, "Since we carry the man where he wants to go and get him in position to do what the brain wants, we think that we should be boss."

The hands said, "Since we do all of the work and earn all of the money to keep the rest of you going, we should be boss."

The eyes said, "Since we look out for all of you and tell you where danger lurks, we should be boss."

And so it went, the heart, ears, lungs, etc. Finally the asshole spoke up and demanded that it be made boss. All of the other parts laughed at the idea of the asshole being boss.

The asshole was so angered that he blocked himself off and refused to function.

Soon the brain was feverish, the eyes crossed and ached, the feet were too weak to walk, the hands hung limply at the sides, the lungs and heart struggled to keep going. All of them pleaded with the brain to relent and let the asshole be boss.

And so it happened. All of the other parts did the work and the asshole just bossed and passed a lot of crap.

The moral of the story:

You don't have to be a brain to be the boss, just an asshole.

MEN HAVE USELESS PARTS

* He has an Adams apple that isn't an apple

* Two calves that will never become cows

* A nose bridge that doesn't lead anywhere

* A roof of the mouth that won't cover anything

* Twenty nails that won't hold a board

* A chest that won't hold linen

* Two tits that won't give milk

* Two buns that won't feed anyone

* A belly button that won't button

* Two balls that won't roll

* An ass that won't pull a plow

* An organ that won't play music

* A cock that won't crow

Of course women have a pussy that won't catch mice.

PSYCHIATRY

A man who had been in a mental home for some years finally seemed to have improved to the point where it was thought he might be released.

The head psychiatrist of the institution, in a fit of commendable caution, decided to have one final interview with him.

"If we release you, as we are considering, what do you intend to do with your life?"

The inmate said, "It would be wonderful to get back to real life and if I do, I will certainly refrain from making my former mistake. I was a nuclear physicist you know, and it was the stress of my work in weapons research that helped put me here. If I am released, I shall confine myself to work in pure theory, where I trust the situation will be less difficult and stressful."

"Marvelous," said the head of the institution.

"Or else, I might teach. There is something to be said for spending one's life in bringing up a new generation of scientists."

"Absolutely," said the doctor.

"Then again, I might write. There is considerable need for books on science for the general public. I might even write a novel based on my experiences in this fine institution."

"An interesting possibility," nodded the doctor.

"And finally, if none of these things appeals to me, I can always continue to be a tea kettle."

EARS

A man lost both ears in an accident. No plastic surgeon could offer him a solution.

He heard of a very good one in Sweden, and went to him. The new surgeon examined him, thought a while, and said, “Yes, I can fix your problem.”

After the operation, he gets the bandages off and the stitches out, then he goes to his hotel. When he wakes up the next morning, he is in a rage and calls his surgeon.

He gets the doctor on the phone and yells, “You swine, you gave me a woman’s ears.”

“Sir, an ear is an ear. What seems to be the problem? Can’t you hear anything with your new ears?”

“You are completely wrong. I hear everything, but I don’t understand a thing.”

CHEAP ADVICE

A man went to a psychiatrist.

"Doc," he said, "I have a problem. Every time I get into bed, I think there's somebody under it. I get under the bed and I think there's somebody on top of it. Top, under, top, under. You must help me. I'm going crazy."

"Just put yourself in my hands for two years," said the shrink. "Come to me three times a week, and I'll cure your fears."

"How much do you charge?"

"A hundred dollars per visit."

"I'll think about it," said the man.

Six months later the doctor met the guy on the street. "Why didn't you ever come to see me again?" asked the psychiatrist.

"For a hundred buck's a visit? A bartender cured me for ten dollars."

"Is that so? How did he cure you?"

"He told me to cut the legs off the bed."

ANATOMY

The teacher was telling her students in the sex education class about human anatomy.

She took her pointer and pointed to the picture of the female and said, “The female has two breasts and one vagina.”

She then pointed to the male picture and said, “The male has one penis.”

Terrible Tommy jumped up from his seat and said, “That’s wrong teacher.”

“Why do you think I am wrong, Tommy?” begged the teacher.

My daddy has two of them,” explained Terrible Tommy. “One that’s about three inches long that he pees with, and another one that’s about eight inches long that he brushes the babysitter’s teeth with.”

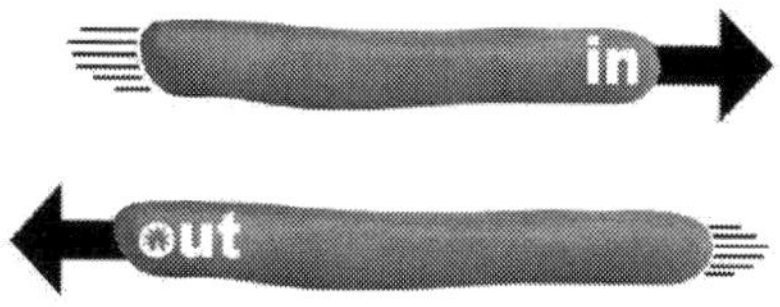

MY THING

My nookie days are over.
My pilot light is out.
What used to be my sex appeal
Is just my water spout.

Time was, when, on its own
From my trousers it would spring.
But now I have a full time job
To find the blessed thing.

I used to be embarrassed
To make the thing behave
For every single morning
It used to watch me shave.

But now I'm getting older
It sure gives me the blues
To see the thing hang down its head
And watch me shine my shoes.

EYES

An airline pilot with poor eyesight had managed to pass his periodic vision exams by memorizing the eye charts beforehand.

One year his doctor used a new chart that the pilot had never before seen. The pilot proceeded to recite the old chart and the doctor realized that she had been hoodwinked.

The pilot proved to be nearly blind as a bat, but the doctor could not contain her curiosity. “How is it that someone with your eyesight can manage to pilot a plane at all? I mean, how for example do you taxi the plane out to the runway?”

The pilot said, “It’s really not very difficult. All you have to do is follow the instructions of the ground controller over the radio. And the landmarks have all become quite familiar to me over the years.”

“I can understand that, but what about the take-off?”

“Again, a simple procedure. I just aim the plane down the runway, go to full throttle, pull back on the stick, and off we go.”

“But once you’re aloft?”

“Everything’s fully automated these days. The flight computer knows our destination, I hit the autopilot switch and the plane pretty much flies itself.”

“But I still don’t understand how you could possibly land.”

“That’s the easiest part, I use the airport’s radio beacon to get us on the proper glide path. Then I just throttle down and wait for the co-pilot to yell, ‘AIEEEE!’ Then I pull the nose up, and the plane lands just fine.”

ANSWERING SERVICE

The following is a transcript of the new answering service recently installed at a mental health institute.

Hello, and welcome to the mental health hotline.

If you are obsessive-compulsive, press 1 repeatedly.

If you are co-dependent, please ask someone to press 2 for you.

If you have multiple personalities, press 3, 4, 5, and 6.

If you are paranoid, we know who you are and what you want. Stay on the line so we can trace your call.

If you are delusional, press 7 and your call will be transferred to the mother ship.

If you are schizophrenic, listen carefully and a small voice will tell you which number to press.

If you are a manic-depressive, it doesn't matter which number you press - no one will answer.

If you are dyslexic, press 9696969.

If you have a nervous disorder, please fidget with the hash key until a representative comes on the line.

If you have amnesia press 8 and state your name, address, phone number, date of birth, social security number, and your mother's maiden name.

If you have post-traumatic stress disorder, slowly and carefully press 000.

If you have bi-polar disorder, please leave a message after the beep or before the beep, or after the beep. Please wait for the beep.

If you have short-term memory loss, press 9.

If you have short-term memory loss, press 9.

If you have short-term memory loss, press 9.

If you have short-term memory loss, press 9.

If you have low self esteem. Please hang up. All our operators are too busy to talk to you.

DIMUNITIVE PENIS

187 Slimey Slew Dr.

Upper Thighs, U R 00122

Dear Mr. Dillywhacker;

We sincerely regret to inform you that we must reject your recent application to model our 'Dimumitive Dodo' style, one-inch condom.

Our Board of Directors had decided that, although your physical attributes, other than the penile region, are not unpleasant to observe, the picture of you wearing our product is not the most pleasing image that we strive to portray to the public.

A loose condom that is portrayed as baggy and wrinkled, even in the best of circumstances, is not altogether romantic.

Your suggestions to fill the void with silly putty or polygrip were good ones. However, they have proven to be too lumpy and tend to fall out at the most inopportune moments. Should we decide to market an even smaller version in the future, rest assured that we will contact you.

Wishing you continued pleasure,

Dick Abundance

Chairman, Acme Condoms

BREASTS AND THINGS

A family is at the dinner table and the son asks his father, “Dad, how many kinds of boobies are there?”

The father is a bit surprised by the question, but answers, “Well son, there are three kinds of breasts. In her twenties, a woman’s breasts are like melons, round and firm.

In her thirties to forties, her breasts are like pears, still nice but hanging a bit.

After fifty, her breasts are like onions.”

“Onions?”

“Yes, you look at them and they make you cry.”

This infuriated his wife and daughter so the daughter asks, “Mom, how many kinds of thingies are there?”

The mother smiles and answers, “Well dear, a man goes through three phases. In his twenties, his thingie is like an oak tree, mighty and hard.

In his thirties and forties, it is like a birch, flexible but reliable.

After his fifties, it is like a Christmas tree.”

“A Christmas tree?”

“Yes, dead from the roots up and the balls are for decoration only.”

THERAPY

A middle-aged businessman took a young woman half his age as his wife. The fantasy of having a young woman in his bed soon became a nightmare when he found that he could not last long enough to satisfy his young bride.

His wife, as understanding as she was exciting, told him that all was well even if he was quick to get out of the saddle.

Determined to satisfy this sweet young thing, the man visited the doctor to get some advice.

"Doctor, I can't seem to hold back for very long when I make love to my young wife and I can't satisfy her. What can I do?"

The doctor smiled, patted him on the shoulder, and said in a professional manner, "Try a bit of self-stimulation before having intercourse with your wife and you'll find that you'll last longer and ultimately satisfy her."

"OK, doctor, if you think that will help."

Later that afternoon, his young bride called him at work to let him know that she would be attacking him at the front door when he arrived home.

"Be prepared, my darling. I'm going to ravish you," she cooed over the phone.

The man decided to follow the doctor's advice, but couldn't decide where. In the office? The copy room? What if someone walked in on him?

He got in his truck and began the journey home. Soon he decided he would find a spot on the road to pull over, climb underneath the truck, and pretend to be inspecting the rear axle, and do the deed there.

A moment later, he pulled over, crawled beneath the truck, closed his eyes tightly, fantasized about his young wife, and began his therapy.

A few minutes later, just as he was about to complete his therapy session, he felt someone tugging on his pants leg. Keeping his eyes tightly shut to avoid ruining the fantasy he was enjoying, he said, "Yes?"

"Sir, I'm with the Police Department. Could you tell me what you are doing, please?" said the officer.

"Yes, officer, I'm inspecting my truck's rear axle," he replied confidently.

"Well, you might check the brakes while you're down there. Your truck rolled down the hill a few minutes ago."

GOD AND BRAINS

The teacher was trying to explain evolution to her young students.

Teacher - Tommy do you see the tree outside?
Tommy - Yes.
Tommy, do you see the grass outside?
Yes.
Go outside and look up and see if you can see the sky.
(Upon his return) Yes, I saw the sky.
Did you see God up there?
No.
That's my point. We can't see God because he isn't there. Possibly he just does not exist.

Lisa spoke up and wanted to ask Tommy some questions. The teacher agreed.

Lisa - Tommy, did you see the tree outside?
Tommy - Yes.
Tommy, did you see the grass outside?
Yes.
Did you see the sky?
Yes.
Do you see the teacher?
Yes.
Do you see her brain?
No.
Then according to what we were taught today in school, she may not even have a brain.

MISSING PARTS

A man is waiting for his wife to give birth. The doctor comes in and informs the dad that his son was born without torso, arms, or legs. The son is just a head. Nevertheless, the dad loves his son and raises him as well as he can, with love and compassion.

After twenty-one years, the son is now old enough for his first drink. Dad takes him to the bar and tearfully tells the son he is proud of him. He orders up the biggest, strongest drink for his boy. With all the bar patrons looking on curiously and the bartender looking in disbelief, the boy takes his first sip of alcohol.

Swoop! A torso pops out.

The shocked father begs his son to drink again.

The patrons chant, "Take another drink."

Swoop! Two arms pop out.

The gang goes wild. The father is crying and wailing, and begs his son on to drink again.

The patrons chant, "Take another drink."

By now the boy is getting tipsy, and with his new hands he reaches down, grabs his drink, and guzzles the last of it.

Swoop! Two legs pop out.

The place is in chaos. The father falls to his knees and thanks God.

The boy stands up on his new legs and stumbles to the left, then to the right, right through the front door and into the street, where a truck runs over him and kills him instantly.

The group falls silent. The father moans in grief. The bartender sighs and says, "He should have quit drinking while he was still a head."

THE EXAM

Tony Duminski, Aarne Elias, and Frank Cavanaugh, three patients in a mental institution, prepare for an examination given by the head psychiatrist.

If the patients pass the exam, they will be free to leave the hospital. However, if they fail, the institution will detain them for another five years.

The doctor takes the three patients to the top of a diving board looking over an empty swimming pool, and asks the patients to fly like a Cardinal over the pool.

Tony jumps head first into the pool and breaks both arms.

Then Aarne jumps and breaks both legs.

Frank, the third patient, looks over the side and refuses to jump.

“Congratulations. You’re a free man. Just tell me why you didn’t jump?” asked the doctor.

Frank answered, “I can’t swim.”

MUFFS

Seven wise men truly inspired
Shared an idea uniquely desired.
The first was a carpenter, full of wit
With a hammer and chisel, he made the split.
The second was a blacksmith, black as coal
With anvil and sledge, he made the hole.
The third was a tailor, long and slim
With a piece of red ribbon, he lined it within.
The fourth was a furrier, big and stout
With the skin of a bear, he lined it without.
The fifth was a fisherman, old and bent
With a rotten old fish, he gave it a scent.
The sixth was a preacher, with a Theo degree
With his hand he touched it and said it would pee.
The last was a swinger, both eager and tough
He played with it fondly and named it a muff.

STRESS MANAGEMENT

Just in case you are having a rough day, here is a stress management technique recommended in all the latest psychological journals. The funny thing is that it really does work.

Picture yourself lying on your belly on a warm rock that hangs out over a crystal clear stream.

Picture yourself with both your hands dangling in the cool running water.

Birds are sweetly singing in the cool mountain air.

No one knows your secret place.

You are in total seclusion from that hectic place called the world.

The soothing sound of a gentle waterfall fills the air with a cascade of serenity.

The water is so crystal clear that you can easily make out the face of the person you are holding underwater.

It does work, I see you smiling.

Ageing

SENIOR BITS

Age is a very high price to pay for maturity.

~ ~

'Long in the tooth' means old. This was originally used to describe old horses. As horses age, their gums recede, giving the impression that their teeth are growing. Hence, the longer the teeth look, the older the horse.

~ ~

I am not old, I am chronologically gifted.

~ ~

Four Stages of Life

~ ~

Campbells has come out with a new soup for seniors. It has extra large letter noodles.

~ ~

Doctor: "I have very bad news. You have cancer and Alzheimer's."
Patient: "Well, at least I don't have cancer."

~ ~

'No spring chicken' means you are old or at least not young anymore. This saying has its origins back when there were no incubators or warm hen houses.

Chicks could not be raised during winter and New England growers found that those born in the spring brought premium prices in the summer market places. When they tried to pass off old birds as part of the spring crop, smart buyers would protest that the bird was 'no spring chicken'.

~ ~

Old age is the time when actions creak louder than words.

~ ~

One day, I passed by a nursing home while walking to the store. On the front lawn were six old ladies laying naked on the grass. I thought this was a bit unusual, but continued on my way to the store.

On my return trip, I passed the same nursing home and the same six ladies were lying naked on the lawn. This time my curiosity got the best of me, so I went inside to talk to the administrator.

"Do you know there are six ladies lying naked on your front lawn?"

He replied, "Yes, they're retired prostitutes and they are having a yard sale."

~ ~

Pain and suffering are inevitable, but misery is optional.

~ ~

Young folks need to learn that old folks know more about being young than young folks know about being old.

~ ~

What's the best form of birth control after age fifty?
Nudity.

~ ~

A little old lady was walking up and down the halls in a nursing home. As she walked, she flipped up her nightgown and said, "Supersex."

She walked up to an old man, flipped her gown at him, grinned, and said, "Supersex."

The old man was silent for a moment, and finally answered, "I'll take the soup."

~ ~

Yes, that was very loud Mr. Meiers, but I said I wanted to hear your heart.

~ ~

Middle age is when you choose cereal for the fiber and not the toy.

~ ~

An elderly man went to his doctor and said, “Doc, I think I’m getting senile. Several times lately, I have forgotten to zip up.”

“That’s not senility,” replied the doctor. “Senility is when you forget to zip down.”

~ ~

Retirement is the best medicine.

~ ~

A recent study has revealed alarming statistics that suggest senior citizens are the now biggest carriers of AIDS.

Hearing AIDS
Seeing AIDS
Chewing AIDS
Band AIDS
RolAIDS
Walking AIDS
MedicAIDS
Government AIDS.

~ ~

Aunt Eleanor went to her doctor to see what could be done about her troublesome constipation. “It’s terrible,” she said to the doctor. “I haven’t moved my bowels in more than a week.”

“I see. Have you done anything about it?” asked the doctor.

“Oh, yes,” Aunt Eleanor replied, “I sit in the bathroom for a good half hour in the morning and then again at night.”

“No,” said the doctor, “I mean do you take anything?”

“Of course I do,” she answered, “I take a magazine.”

~ ~

Seven Dwarves of Menopause

Itchy, Bitchy, Sweaty, Sleepy, Bloated, Forgetful & Psycho

~ ~

What is the number one cause of diarrhea in nursing homes?
Constipation

~ ~

A little old lady goes to the doctor and says, "Doctor I have this problem with gas, but it really doesn't bother me too much. They never smell and are always silent. As a matter of fact, I farted at least ten times since I have been here in your office. You didn't know I was farting because they don't smell and are silent."

The doctor says, "I see, take these pills and come back to see me next week."

The next week the lady goes back and tells the doctor, "I don't know what the hell you gave me, but now my farts although still silent, stink terribly."

The doctor says, "Good. Now that we have cleared up your sinuses, let's work on your hearing."

~ ~

It is well documented that for every mile that you jog, you add one minute to your life. This enables you, at eighty five years old, to spend an additional five months in a nursing home at ten thousand dollars per month.

~ ~

During a routine physical exam, ninety-year old man said to his doctor, "I've never felt better. I have an eighteen-year old bride who is pregnant with my child. What do you think of that?"

The doctor replied, "I have an elderly friend who is a hunter and never misses a season. One day he was in a hurry and picked up his umbrella instead of his gun by mistake. When he got to the creek, he saw a beaver. He raised his umbrella and went bang, bang, and the beaver fell dead. What do you think of that?"

The ninety-year old said, "I'd say somebody else shot the beaver."

The doctor said, "My point exactly."

~ ~

A tough old cowboy once counseled his grandson that if he wanted to live a long life, the secret was to sprinkle a little gunpowder on his oatmeal every morning.

The grandson did this and he lived to the age of ninety-three.

When he died, he left fourteen children, twenty eight grandchildren, thirty five great grandchildren, and a fifteen foot hole in the wall of the crematorium.

~ ~

An elderly couple was attending church services when, about halfway through she leans over and says to him, "I just had a silent passing of gas, what do you think I should do?"

He leans over and replies, "Put a new battery in your hearing aid."

~ ~

Two elderly gentlemen were sitting on a bench at the retirement center and one turns to the other and says, "I'm 92 years old and full of aches and pains. I know you are about my age, how do you feel?"
The other responds, "I feel like a newborn baby."
"Do you really feel that good?"
"Yep, no hair, no teeth, and I think I just wet my pants."

~ ~

Three old ladies named were sitting on a park bench having a quiet conversation when a flasher approached from across the park. The flasher came up to the ladies, stood right in front of them and opened his trench coat.

Marion immediately had a stroke.

Then Helen also had a stroke.

But Eleanor, being more feeble, couldn't reach that far.

~ ~

A senior citizen visits his doctor for a routine check-up and everything seems fine. The doctor asks him about his sex life.

The man drawled, "Not bad at all to be honest. The wife ain't all that interested anymore, so I just cruise around. In the past week I was able to pick-up and bed at least three girls, none of whom were over thirty years old."

"My goodness Jack, and at your age too," the doctor said.

"I hope you took at least some precautions."

"Yep. I may be old, but I ain't senile. I gave them all a phony name."

~ ~

I think the life cycle is all backwards.
- You should start out dead and get it out of the way.
- Then, you wake up in an old age home feeling better every day.
- You get kicked out for being too healthy; go collect your pension, and then when you start work, you get a gold watch on your first day.
- You work forty years until you're young enough to enjoy your retirement.
- You drink alcohol, you party, you're generally promiscuous, and you get ready for High School.
- You go to primary school, you become a kid, you play, you have no responsibilities, you become a baby, and then. . .
- You spend your last nine months floating peacefully in luxury, in spa-like conditions; central heating, room service on tap, larger quarters every day, and then. . . *you finish off as an orgasm.*

~ ~

Two elderly residents, Mike and Karen, were sitting alone in the lobby of their nursing home one evening. Mike looked over and said to Karen, “I know just what you want. For five dollars I’ll have sex with you right over there in that rocking chair.”

Ms. Nosser looked surprised, but didn’t say a word.

Mike continued, “For ten dollars, I’ll do it with you on that nice soft sofa over there, but for twenty dollars I’ll take you back to my room, light some candles, and give you the most romantic evening you have ever had in your life.”

Karen fixed her red hair, but still said nothing. After a few minutes, she started digging down in her purse. She pulled out a wrinkled twenty dollar bill and held it up.

“So you want the nice romantic evening in my room,” said Mike, “Hallelujah!”

“Get serious,” Karen replied. “I want it four times in the rocking chair.”

~ ~

Nine oldsters booted out of nursing home — for trying to have an orgy!

LONDON — A group of nine love-hungry codgers were booted out of an old folks' home — after they tried to have an orgy in the recreation room!

The unidentified oldsters, who ranged in age from 73 to 98, had apparently planned the unauthorized after-hours get-together for weeks, according to Melinda Helterford, spokesperson for the well-respected Edith Scarborough Nursing Home.

"They somehow got it in their heads to celebrate the 90th birthday of one of the women with a kind of sex party," said Miss Helterford.

"This may sound harmless or amusing to some people, but Scarborough has a reputation to uphold. We cannot tolerate that kind of conduct."

By MIKE FOSTER
Weekly World News

The nursing home made a concerted effort to keep the bizarre story out of the press and so details are difficult to come by.

But according to British papers, the let-it-all-hang-out party took place just after midnight on October 28. The three wrinkly Romeos and six sagging seductresses gathered together in the rec room and stripped to the buff.

"They really set the scene," a nursing home staffer who was not identified told a London tabloid. "They'd got their hands on candles, which they lit, and even put on music to create a sexy mood."

The nude geezer gala went on for about 20 minutes before orderlies heard rumba music coming from the recreational room and went to investigate.

When they opened the doors, they were shocked to find the old-timers crowded together in their birthday suits, slathered with baby oil.

"They hadn't got too far — I guess it was taking some of the gents a while to get started," the staffer said.

"But they were all naked. Believe me, it was the scariest thing I've seen in my life."

~ ~

LONG LIFE

I recently picked a new primary care physician. After two visits and exhaustive lab tests, he said I was doing fairly well for my age.

A little concerned about the comment, I couldn't resist asking him, "Do you think I will live to be eighty?"

He asked, "Do you smoke tobacco or drink beer?"

"No," I replied, "I have never done either."

Then he asked, "Do you eat rib-eye steaks and barbeque ribs?"

I said, "No, I heard that all red meat is very unhealthy."

"Do you spend a lot of time in the sun, like playing golf?" he asked.

"No I don't," I said.

He said, "Do you gamble, drive fast cars, or fool around with sexy women?"

"No," I said, "I have never done any of those things."

He looked at me and said, "Then why in heck do you want to live to be eighty?"

LONG TERM CARE

One morning, the residents of a long-term care facility were heading toward the dining room for breakfast. Joe came running up to Herman, who sat patiently in his wheelchair. "Herman, Herman," exclaimed Joe, "It's my birthday today. Guess how old I am."

"I don't want to guess," said Herman. "Just tell me how old you are."

"No, that's no fun," replied Joe. "Guess how old I am."

"Seventy."

"Nope."

"I give up, Joe. How old are you?" asked Herman.

"I'm seventy-eight years old today." exclaimed Joe proudly.

Off he tottered down the hall, with a bounce in his step. He ran up to Gladys and asked her to guess how old he was.

"I won't guess," said Gladys, "But if you want me to tell you exactly how old you are, just unzip your pants and I'll tell you exactly."

Joe looked at her with a shocked expression on his face. He stood there for a minute, shrugged his shoulders, and unzipped his pants.

Gladys reached into his pants with her left hand, played around in there for a little bit, smiled, and withdrew her hand. "You're seventy-eight years old today," she exclaimed.

Joe looked at her and asked, "How in the world did you figure that out?"

"I didn't," smirked Gladys. "I overheard you tell Herman when you were down the hall."

MEDICAL EXAM

An elderly married couple scheduled their annual medical examination the same day so they could travel together.

After the husband's examination, the doctor then said to him, "You appear to be in good health. Do you have any medical concerns that you would like to discuss with me?"

"In fact, I do," said the man. "After I have sex with my wife for the first time, I am usually hot and sweaty. And then, after I have sex with my wife the second time, I am usually cold and chilly."

"This is very interesting," replied the doctor. "Let me do some research and get back to you."

After examining the elderly wife, the doctor said to her, "Everything appears to be fine. Do you have any medical concerns that you would like to discuss with me?"

The lady replied that she had no questions or concerns.

The doctor then asked, "Your husband had an unusual concern. He claims that he is usually hot and sweaty after having sex the first time with you and then cold and chilly after the second time. Do you know why?"

"Oh that old buzzard." she replied. "That's because the first time is usually in July and the second time is usually in December."

MEMORY LAPSES

A couple in their nineties is having problems remembering things, so they decide to the go the doctor for a checkup. The doctor tells them that they're physically okay, but they might want to start writing things down to help them remember.

While watching TV later that night, the old man gets up from his chair.

His wife asks, "Where are you going?"

"To the kitchen," he replies.

She asks, "Will you get me a bowl of ice cream?"

The husband says, "Sure."

She gently reminds him, "Don't you think you should write it down so you can remember it?"

He says, "No, I can remember ice cream."

She then says, "I would also like some strawberries on top. You better write it down, because I know you'll forget it."

He says, "I can remember that you want a bowl of ice cream with strawberries."

She adds, "I would also like whipped cream. Now I'm certain you'll forget that so you'd better write it down."

He says, "I don't need to write it down. I can remember ice cream with strawberries, and whipped cream." He then grumbles and proceeds to the kitchen.

After twenty minutes the old man returns from the kitchen and hands his wife a plate of bacon and eggs.

She stares at the plate and says, "Where's my toast?"

EUTHANASIA

A vet had been called to examine a ten-year-old Irish Wolfhound named Roger. The dog's owners, Dan, his wife Sally, and their little boy Don, were all very much attached to Roger and they were hoping for a miracle.

The vet examined Roger and found he was dying of cancer. He told the family there were no miracles left for the animal, and offered to perform the euthanasia procedure in their home. As he made arrangements, the parents said they thought it would be good their young child to observe the procedure. They felt he might learn something from the experience.

The next day, Roger's family surrounded him. Don seemed so calm while petting the old dog for the last time, that the vet wondered if he understood what was going on.

Roger quickly slipped peacefully away. The little boy seemed to accept Roger's transition without any difficulty or confusion.

They sat together for a while after Roger's death, wondering aloud about the sad fact that animal lives are shorter than human lives.

Don was listening quietly and said, "I know why."

They all turned to him and heard his comforting explanation.

He said, "People are born so that they can learn how to live a good life, like loving everybody all the time and being nice, right?"

The child continued, "Dogs already know how to do that, so they don't have to stay as long."

MEDICARE

An elderly couple went to the doctor's office. They were escorted to the treatment room and the doctor asked what their problem was.

The old man said, "We want you to observe us having sex to see if we are doing it correctly." The doctor agreed to do this.

After they finished and were dressing he gave them his assurance that everything was satisfactory and charged them forty dollars.

During the next month the old couple came back each week and always had the same request. The doctor obliged but was getting rather curious and asked why they kept coming back when everything always appeared normal in every way.

The old man finally confessed, "It's like this. We're married, but not to each other and so we can't go to my house and we can't go to her house. It would cost us twenty bucks to get a motel. We can come here for forty bucks and Medicare will pay us back thirty so we come out ten bucks ahead."

LONGEVITY

An eighty year old man went to the doctor for a checkup and the doctor was amazed at what good shape the guy was in.

The doctor asked, “To what do you attribute your good health?”

The old timer said, “I’m a golfer and that’s why I’m in such good shape. I am up well before daylight, and out golfing up and down the fairways.”

The doctor said, “I’m sure that helps, but there has to be more to it. How old was your father when he died?”

The old timer said, “Who said my dad’s dead?”

“You mean you’re eighty years old and your dad’s still alive? How old is he?” asked the doctor.

The old timer said, “He’s a hundred and he golfed with me this morning, and that’s why he is still alive, He’s also a golfer.”

The doctor said, “How about your grandfather? How old was he when he died?”

The old timer said, “Who said my grandpa’s dead?”

“Wow, how old is your grandfather?” asked the doctor.

The old timer said, “He’s a hundred and eighteen years old.”

The doctor said, “I guess he went golfing with you this morning too?”

The old timer said, “No, grandpa couldn’t go this morning because he just got married.”

The doctor said in amazement, “Married. Why would a hundred and eighteen year old guy want to get married?”

“Who said he wanted to?” replied the old gent.

AGEING

According to Dr. Seuss

I cannot see

I cannot pee

I cannot chew

I cannot screw

Oh, my God, what can I do?

My memory shrinks

My hearing stinks

No sense of smell

I look like hell

My mood is bad – can you tell?

My body's drooping

Have trouble pooping

The golden years have come at last.

The golden years can kiss my ass!

HYPNOTISM

It was entertainment night at the senior center and the Amazing Leo was topping the bill. People came from miles around to see the famous hypnotist do his stuff.

As Leo went to the front of the meeting room, he announced, "Unlike most hypnotists who invite two or three people up here to be put into a trance, I intend to hypnotize each and every member of the audience."

The excitement was almost electric as Leo withdrew a beautiful antique pocket watch from his coat. "I want you each to keep your eyes on this antique watch. It's a very special watch. It has been in my family for six generations."

He began to swing the watch gently back and forth while quietly chanting, "Watch the watch, watch the watch, watch the watch."

The crowd became mesmerized as the watch swayed back and forth with light gleaming off its polished surface.

Hundreds of pairs of eyes followed the swaying watch, until suddenly, it slipped from the hypnotist's fingers, fell to the floor and broke into a hundred pieces.

"Shit!" said the hypnotist.

It took three days to clean up the senior center.

THE PHYSICAL

Seventy-year-old Tim went for his annual physical. All of his tests came back with normal results.

Doctor Achen said, "Tim, everything looks great physically. How are you doing mentally and emotionally? Are you at peace with yourself, and do you have a good relationship with your God?"

Tim replied, "God and me are tight. He knows I have poor eyesight, so He's fixed it so that when I get up in the middle of the night to go to the bathroom, poof, the light goes on when I pee, and then poof, the light goes off when I'm done."

"Wow," commented Doctor Achen, "That's incredible."

A little later in the day Doctor Achen called Tim's wife. "Mary," he said, "Tim is just fine. However, I had to call because I am in awe of his relationship with God. Is it true that he gets up during the night and the light goes on in the bathroom and then poof, the light goes off?"

Mary exclaimed, "That old fool. He's peeing in the refrigerator again."

3 Rules of Getting Older

Never pass a bathroom,
don't waste a hard-on,
and never trust a fart

FLATULENCE

The family wheeled grandma in her wheelchair, out on the lawn where the activities for her hundredth birthday were taking place.

Grandma couldn't speak very well, but she could write notes when she needed to communicate.

After a short time out on the lawn, grandma started leaning off to the right, so some family members grabbed her, straightened her up, and stuffed pillows on her right.

A short time later, she started leaning off to her left, so again the family grabbed her and stuffed pillows on her left.

Soon she started leaning forward, so the family members again grabbed her, and then tied a pillowcase around her waist to hold her up.

A nephew, who arrived late, came running up to grandma and said, "Hi grandma, you're looking good. How are they treating you?"

Grandma took out her little notepad and slowly wrote a note to the nephew, "Fine, but I wish they'd just let me fart once in a while."

DISEASE OF AGE

Seward is ninety five and lives in a senior citizen home. Every night after dinner, Seward goes to a secluded garden behind the center to sit and ponder his accomplishments and long life.

One evening, Emma, age eighty-eight, wanders into the garden. They begin to chat and before they know it, several hours have passed. After a short lull in their conversation, Seward turns to Emma and asks, "Do you know what I miss most of all?"

She asks, "What?"

He replies, "Sex."

Emma exclaims, "Why you old fart, you couldn't get it up if I held a gun to your head."

"I know, but it would be nice if a woman just held it for a while."

"I can oblige," says Emma. She gently unzips his trousers and removes his manhood and proceeds to hold it. Afterward, they agree to meet secretly each night in the garden where they would sit and talk and Emma would hold his manhood.

One night, Seward didn't show up at their usual meeting place.

Emma was worried and decided to find him and make sure that he was still alive. She walked around the home until she found him sitting by the pool with another female resident, who was holding Seward's manhood.

Emma was furious and yelled, "You two-timing creep. What does she have that I don't have?"

Seward smiled and replied, "Parkinson's"

NURSING HOMES

About two years ago my wife and I were on a cruise through the western Mediterranean aboard a Princess liner. At dinner we noticed an elderly lady sitting alone along the rail of the grand stairway in the main dining room. I also noticed that all the staff, ships officers, waiters, busboys, etc., seemed very familiar with this lady.

I asked our waiter who the lady was, expecting to be told she owned the line. He said she was a regular passenger and had been on board for the last four cruises, in a row.

As we left the dining room one evening I caught her eye and stopped to say hello. We chatted and I said, "I understand you've been on this ship for the last four cruises."

She replied, "Yes, that's true."

I stated, "I don't understand, are the cruises that good?"

She replied, "It's cheaper than a nursing home."

She convinced me. I have decided that there will be no nursing home in my future. When I get old and feeble, I am going to get on a Princess Cruise Ship. The average cost for a nursing home is two hundred dollars per day.

I have checked on reservations at Princess and I can get a long-term discount and senior discount price of about a hundred fifty per day. That leaves $50 a day for other things.

Gratuities will be only $10 per day.

I will have as many as ten meals a day if I can waddle to the restaurant, or I can have room service. This means I can have breakfast in bed every day of the week.

Princess has as many as three swimming pools, a workout room, free washers and dryers, and shows every night.

They have free toothpaste and razors, and free soap and shampoo.

They will even treat you like a customer, not a patient. An extra five dollars worth of tips will have the entire staff scrambling to help you.

I will get to meet new people every week.

TV broken, light bulb needs changing, need to have the mattress replaced? No problem. They will fix everything and apologize to you for your inconvenience.

Clean sheets and towels every day, and you don't even have to ask for them.

If you fall in the nursing home and break a hip you are on Medicare. If you fall and break a hip on the Princess ship they will upgrade you to a suite for the rest of your life.

Hold on for the best part. Do you want to see South America, the Panama Canal, Tahiti, Australia, New Zealand, Asia, or anywhere else you want to go? Princess will have a ship ready to go.

Don't look for me in a nursing home, just call shore to ship.

Best of all, when you die, there are no funeral expenses. They dump you over the side at no extra charge.

SENIOR CENTER

Maude and Mabel lived next door to each other for over forty years, and over the years became close friends. One day Maude came to Mabel and said, "These houses are becoming too much for us, let's sell them and move into rest homes where people will take care of us."

The two little old ladies each went to a different nursing home. It was not long before Maude felt very lonesome for Mabel, so one day she asked to be driven to the Jewish Home to visit her old friend. When she arrived, she was greeted with open arms, hugs, and kisses. Maude said, "Mabel, how you like it here?"

Mabel went on and on about the wonderful food, the facility, and the care takers. Then, with a twinkle in her eye, she said, "But the best thing is that I now have a boyfriend."

Maude said, "Now isn't that wonderful. Tell me all about it."

Mabel said, "After lunch we go up to my room and sit on the edge of the bed. I let him touch me on the top, and then on the bottom, and then we sing Jewish songs."

Maude said, "For sure it's a blessing. I'm so glad for you."

Mabel said, "And how is it with you, Maude?"

Maude said it was also wonderful at her new facility, and that she also had a boyfriend.

Mabel said, "Good for you. So what do you do?"

"We also go up to my room after lunch and sit on the edge of the bed. I let him touch me on top, and then I let him touch me down below."

Mabel said, "Yes, and then?"

Maude said, "Well, since we don't know any songs, we just screw."

PROTECTION

Two old ladies were outside their nursing home, having a smoke when it started to rain.

One of the ladies pulled out a condom, cut off the end, put it over her cigarette, and continued smoking.

Lisa said, "What is that?"

Lucy replied, "A condom. This way my cigarette doesn't get wet."

Lisa asked, "Where did you get it?"

Lucy said, "You can get them at any drugstore."

The next day, Lisa hobbles herself to the local drugstore and announces to the pharmacist that she wants a box of condoms.

The guy is a little bit embarrassed and looked at her kind of strangely. He could tell that she was well past her prime, but he asked what brand she preferred.

Lisa said, "It doesn't matter son, as long as it fits a Camel."

The pharmacist fainted.

ARTHRITIS

An old geezer in the retirement home took a fancy to an old lady who is also staying at the home. One day he works up enough courage to tell her he wants to make love to her.

She agrees and suggests that when everyone else is gone for a day trip, they will stay behind and get to it.

He goes to her room on the day and asks her how she likes it.

She says, "I used to like it when a man went down on me."

He says he would love to and goes for it.

After about thirty seconds he comes back up and says, "I'm sorry. I'm afraid I just can't go on. It smells rotten down there."

She says, "It must be my arthritis."

He looks at her and says, "Surely you can't get arthritis down there. And even if you could, it wouldn't cause that horrible smell."

She says, "My arthritis is in my shoulder and I can't wipe my butt.

WHEEL CHAIRS

An old lady in a nursing home is wheeling up and down the halls in her wheelchair making sounds like she's driving a car. As she's going down the hall an old man jumps out of a room and says, "Excuse me madam but you were speeding. Can I see your driver's license?"

She digs around in her purse a little, pulls out a candy wrapper, and hands it to him.

He looks it over, gives her a warning, and sends her on her way.

Up and down the halls she goes again. Again, the same old man jumps out of a room and says, "Excuse me madam but I saw you cross over the center line back there. Can I see your registration please?"

She digs around in her purse a little, pulls out a store receipt, and hands it to him.

He looks it over, gives her another warning, and sends her on her way.

She zooms off again up and down the halls weaving all over. As she comes to the old man's room again he jumps out. He's stark naked and has an erection.

The old lady in the wheel chair looks up and says, "Oh no-not the breathalyzer again."

AGELESS THERAPY

After forty years of marriage, Frankenstein and the Bride of Frankenstein came to a standstill in their love life. Each night Frankenstein would come home from work, eat his dinner, and sit in front of the television set until he fell asleep. Dissatisfied with this arrangement, the bride decided to see a sex therapist.

"He's never in the mood," complained the Bride.

"Try a romantic candlelight dinner," suggested the therapist.

The next day, the bride returned to the therapist with a frown on her face.

"He's still not in the mood," she complained.

"This time," the therapist recommended, "Try something more seductive. Put on some sexy lingerie and lure him into the bedroom."

The bride returned to the therapist the following day complaining that her monster of a husband was still not in the mood.

As a final piece of advice, the therapist said, "You should try to re-create the moment that first sparked your romance."

The next day the bride returned with a huge smile on her face. "Thank you so much," she said to the therapist. "Last night, I forced Frankenstein to come outside in the middle of a lightening storm. And right there, in our backyard, he made love to me like it was our very first time."

"Making love in a lightening storm put him in the mood?" asked the therapist.

"Well," she giggled, "I tied a kite to his penis."

MORGUE

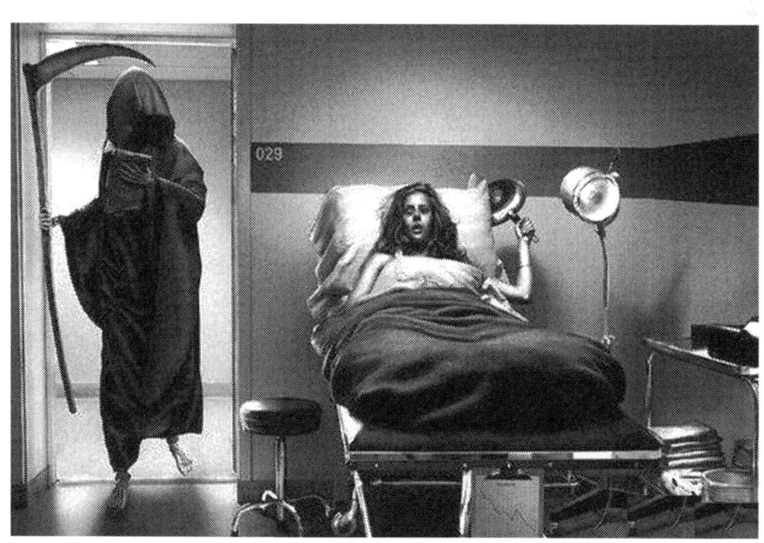

MORGUE DROPPINGS

Never take life seriously. Nobody gets out alive, anyway.

✧ ✧ ✧

✧ ✧ ✧

A 34-year-old white male found dead in the basement of his home died of suffocation, according to police. He was approximately 6’ 2” tall and weighed 225 pounds. He was wearing a pleated skirt, white bra, black and white saddle shoes, and a woman’s wig. It appeared that he was trying to create a schoolgirl’s uniform look. He was also wearing a military gas mask that had the filter canister removed and a rubber hose attached in its place. The other end of the hose was connected to one end of a hollow tube approx. 30” long and 3” in diameter. The tube’s other end was, for reasons unknown, inserted into his rectum and was the cause of his suffocation. Police found the task of explaining the circumstances of his death to his family very awkward.

A mortician was laying out the body of a man with an unbelievably long penis. He called in his receptionist to show her.

She took one look and said, “It’s just like my husband’s penis.”

“Wow, you mean he has one that long?” the mortician asked.

“No,” she replied. “That dead.”

It is a well-known fact that a deceased body harms the mind.

With all the sadness and trauma going on in the world at the moment, it is worth reflecting on the death of a very important person which almost went un-noticed last week. The man who wrote 'The Hokey Pokey' died peacefully at age ninety-three. The most traumatic part for his family was getting him into the coffin.
They put his left leg in. . . and then the trouble started.

Health is merely the slowest possible rate at which one can die.

A funeral service is being held for a woman who has just passed away. At the end of the service the pallbearers are carrying the casket out when they accidentally bump into a wall, and dent the casket.

They hear a faint moan from inside, so they open the casket and find that the woman is actually alive. She lives for ten more years, and then finally dies.

A ceremony is again held at the same place. At the end of the ceremony the pallbearers are again carrying out the casket. As they are walking along, the husband cries out, "Watch out for the damn wall!"

Why do they use sterilized needles for death by lethal injection?

Epitaph: In memory of my father, gone to join his appendix, his tonsils, his olfactory nerve, a kidney, an eardrum, and a leg prematurely removed by an intern who needed the experience.

He's not dead, he's electroencephalographically challenged.

The doctor called Mrs. Cooney over and gave her the news. "I'm afraid your husband has a very serious illness. In fact, it might be fatal. There are two things you have to do to save his life. First, you'll have to fix him three home-cooked meals a day for the rest of his life. And second, you'll have to make love to him every day without fail."

"I'll break the news to him myself," she said. Stepping across the waiting room to her husband Mrs. Cooney announced, "I'm sorry dear, you're going to die."

A mortician was working late one night and it was his job to examine the dead bodies before they were sent off to be buried or cremated. As he examined the body of Mister Shubnell, who was about to be cremated, he made an amazing discovery. Shubnell had the longest thingie he had ever seen.

The mortician looked down and said, "I'm sorry, Mister Shubnell, but I can't send you off to be cremated with a tremendously huge dongle like this. It has to be saved for posterity."

The coroner used his tools to remove Shubnell's manhood. He stuffed his prize into a briefcase and took it home. The first person he showed it to was his wife. "I have something to show you that you won't believe," he said as he opened up his briefcase.

"Oh my God." the wife screamed, "Shubnell is dead!"

In medical school anatomy class, a medical student was supposed to put a mouse in a mason jar, add chloroform to anesthetize it, then remove the mouse, and open it up to be able to see peristalsis and the heart beating.

His hand was too big to reach into the jar and get the mouse so he called over his lab partner, but by this time the mouse had stopped breathing. He quickly grabbed a length of tubing and put it to the mouse's snout and gave a few small breaths of air.

This was the first successful mouth to mouse resuscitation.

An artist asked the gallery owner if there had been any interest in his paintings on display at that time.

"I have good news and bad news," the owner replied. "The good news is that a gentleman inquired about your work and wondered if it would appreciate in value after your death."

"When I told him it would, he bought all of your paintings."

"That's wonderful," the artist exclaimed.

"What's the bad news?"

"He was your doctor."

Birthdays are good for you. The more you have the longer you live.

✧ ✧ ✧

LIVING WILL

You may want to save this to be put with your important papers.

I, ____________________, being of sound mind and body, do not wish to be kept alive indefinitely by artificial means. Under no circumstances should my fate be put in the hands of goofball politicians who couldn't pass ninth-grade biology if their lives depended on it.

If a reasonable amount of time passes and I fail to sit up and ask for (please initial all that apply):

_________Baileys and coffee,
_________margarita,
_________rum,
_________Better Made potato chips,
_________steak,
_________a remote control,
_________bowl of ice cream,
_________chocolate,
_________sex,

It should be presumed that I won't ever get better. When such a determination is reached, I hereby instruct my appointed person and attending physicians to pull the plug, reel in the tubes, and call it a day.

Under no circumstances shall the members of the Legislature enact a special law to keep me on life-support machinery. It is my wish that these boneheads mind their own damn business, and pay attention instead to the future of the millions of Americans who aren't in a permanent coma.

Signature: ____________________
Date: ____________________
Witness: ____________________

THE CASKET

A well-known cardiologist died, and was given an elaborate funeral. A huge heart covered in flowers stood behind the casket during the service.

Following the eulogy, the heart opened, and the casket rolled inside. The heart then closed, sealing the doctor in the beautiful heart forever.

At that point one of the mourners burst into laughter. When confronted, he said, “I’m sorry, I was just thinking of my own funeral. I’m a gynecologist.”

The proctologist fainted.

LAST WISHES

An old priest lay dying in the hospital. For years, he had faithfully served the people of the nation's capital. He motioned for his nurse to come near.

"Yes, Father?" said the nurse.

"I would really like to see Senators Ted Kennedy and Hillary Clinton before I die," whispers the priest.

"I'll see what I can do, Father," replied the nurse.

The nurse sent the request to the Senate and waited for a response. Soon word arrived, that Senators Kennedy and Clinton would be delighted to visit the priest.

As they went to the hospital, Hillary commented to Teddy, "I don't know why the old priest wants to see us, but it certainly will help our images and might even get me elected President. After all, I'm in it to win it."

Kennedy agreed that it was a good thing.

When they arrived at the priest's room, the priest took Ted's hand in his right hand and Hillary's hand in his left. There was silence and a look of serenity on the old priest's face.

Senator Kennedy says, "Father, of all the people you could have chosen, why did you choose us to be with you as you near the end?"

The old priest quietly replies, "I have always tried to pattern my life after our Lord and Savior Jesus Christ."

"Amen," said Teddy.

"Amen," said Hillary.

The old priest continues, "He died between two lying thieves and I would like to do the same."

IDENTIFYING BODIES

Redneck Bubba died in a fire. He was burnt very badly and the morgue needed someone to identify the body.

His two best friends, Daryl and Gomer were sent for.

Daryl went in and the mortician pulled back the sheet.

Daryl said, “Yup, he burnt pretty bad. Roll him over.”

The mortician rolled him over and Daryl looked and said, “Nope, it ain’t Bubba.”

The mortician thought that was rather strange. Then he brought Gomer in to identify the body.

Gomer took a look at him and said “Yup, he sure is burnt real bad, roll him over.”

The mortician rolled him over and Gomer looked down and said, “No, cain’t be Bubba.”

The mortician asked, “How can you tell that is not Bubba?”

Gomer said, “Bubba had two assholes.”

“What? He had two assholes?” said the mortician.

Fer sure, everyone in town knew he had two assholes. Every time we went to town, folks would say, ‘Here comes Bubba with them two assholes’.”

SUICIDE

At the 1994 annual awards dinner given for Forensic Science, AAFS president Dr. Don Harper Mills astounded his audience with the legal complications of a bizarre death. Here is the story:

On March 23, 1994, the medical examiner viewed the body of Ronald Opus and concluded that he died from a shotgun wound to the head. The decedent had jumped from the top of a ten-story building intending to commit suicide.

He left a note to that effect indicating his despondency. As he fell past the ninth floor, his life was interrupted by a shotgun blast passing through a window, which killed him instantly. Neither the shooter nor the decedent was aware that a safety net had been installed just below at the eighth floor level to protect some building workers and that Ronald Opus would not have been able to complete his suicide the way he had planned.

Ordinarily, Dr. Mills continued, "a person who sets out to commit suicide and ultimately succeeds, even though the mechanism might not be what he intended" is still defined as committing suicide. Mr. Opus was shot on the way to certain death nine stories below at street level, but his suicide attempt probably would not have been successful because of the safety net. This caused the medical examiner to feel that he had a homicide on his hands.

The room on the ninth floor from whence the shotgun blast emanated was occupied by an elderly man and his wife. They were arguing vigorously, and he was threatening her with a shotgun. The man was so upset that when he pulled the trigger he completely missed his wife and the pellets went through the window striking Mr. Opus.

When one intends to kill subject A, but kills subject B in the attempt, one is guilty of the murder of subject B.

When confronted with the murder charge, the old man and his wife were both adamant. They both said they thought the shotgun was unloaded. The old man said it was his long standing habit to threaten his wife with the unloaded shotgun.

He had no intention to murder her. Therefore the killing of Mr. Opus appeared to be an accident, that is, the gun had been accidentally loaded.

The continuing investigation turned up a witness who saw the old couple's son loading the shotgun about six weeks prior to the fatal accident. It transpired that the old lady had cut off her son's financial support and the son, knowing the propensity of his father to use the shotgun threateningly, loaded the gun with the expectation that his father would shoot his mother.

The case now becomes one of murder on the part of the son for the death of Ronald Opus.

Now comes the exquisite twist. Further investigation revealed that the son was in fact Ronald Opus. He had become increasingly despondent over both the loss of his financial support and the failure of his attempt to engineer his mother's murder.

This led him to jump off the ten-story building on March 23rd, only to be killed by a shotgun blast passing through the ninth-story window.

The son had actually murdered himself, so the medical examiner closed the case as a suicide.

Actual welcome mat

TERMINAL ILLNESS

A stingy old lawyer, who had been diagnosed with a terminal illness, was determined to prove wrong the saying, "You can't take it with you."

After much thought and consideration, the old ambulance-chaser finally figured out how to take at least some of his money with him when he died.

He instructed his wife to go to the bank and withdraw enough money to fill two pillow cases. He then directed her to take the bags of money to the attic and leave them directly above his bed.

His plan was that when he passed away, he would reach out and grab the bags on his way to heaven.

Several weeks after the funeral, the deceased lawyer's wife was up in the attic cleaning and came upon the two forgotten pillow cases stuffed with cash.

"Oh, that darned old fool," she exclaimed. "I knew he should have had me put the money in the basement."

PHYSICIAN ENVY

There is a world famous Cardiac Surgeon who suddenly drops dead one day. He goes up to heaven, and is standing at the Pearly Gates looking at the long line of people waiting to get in. The doctor looks to Saint Peter and says, "Hi, my name is Doctor Smith, the world famous Heart Surgeon. Can I come into Heaven?"

Saint Peter replies, "Most likely doc, but everyone in heaven is the same. I will look at my book and decide if you are worthy of coming into Heaven, but right now, you must go to the end of the line."

The doctor goes to the end of the line. Quite some time passes and he is getting rather impatient and keeps looking at his watch. After a time, he walks back to Saint Peter and says to him, "Hey, Pete, I am in a hurry, and since I saved so many lives while I was alive, couldn't I come to the front of the line?"

Saint Peter replies, "Doc, we are all the same here, and time has no meaning. No one in heaven is more special than any other. You will have to go to your place in line and wait like all the rest."

The doctor didn't like it very much, but went to the end of the line.

After some more time passes, the doctor spots an elderly man with long gray hair, a long white lab coat, and a stethoscope hanging around his neck. The doctor sees the old man wave at Saint Peter and walk right into heaven.

The doctor immediately walks up to Saint Peter and exclaims, "I thought everyone was the same here in heaven. Why did you let that doctor in and not me? Surely his deeds could not have been greater than mine."

Saint Peter smiles, looks at the doctor, and says, "Well Doc, you're right, but that man was really God. He just likes to think he's a doctor."

SMILING CORPSES

Three smiling corpses are lying in a morgue in a rural Alabama town, and a detective goes into the coroner's office to determine the causes of death. The coroner points to the first dead man.

"This is Cletus, the lucky SOB," he says. "He died of shock after winning twenty million on the lottery."

He then moves on to the second smiling corpse. "This is Bubba," the coroner says. "He died having oral sex with Trudy-May. First oral sex he ever had."

Finally he moves on to the last smiling corpse. "This is Roscoe, the town idiot," says the coroner. "He died after being struck by lightning."

"Why in heek was the idiot smiling?"

"Oh," says the coroner, "He thought he was having his picture taken."

THE NEWS&OBSERVER

17 REMAIN DEAD IN MORGUE SHOOTING SPREE

FUNERAL ATTENDANCE

It's the final of the Rugby World Cup, and a man makes his way to his seat right at center of the field. He sits down, noticing that the seat next to him is empty.

He leans over and asks his neighbor if someone will be sitting in that seat.

"No," says the neighbor. "The seat is empty."

"This is incredible," said the man. "Who in their right mind would have a great seat like this for final game of the World Cup and not be able to use it?"

The neighbor says, "Actually, the seat belongs to me. I was supposed to come with my wife, but she passed away. This is the first World Cup we haven't been attended together since we got married almost twenty five years ago."

The man says, "Oh, I'm so sorry to hear that. That's terrible, but couldn't you find someone else, a friend, a relative, or even a neighbor to take the seat?"

The man shakes his head and says, "No, they're all attending the funeral."

DEAD
END

ADMINISTRATION

ADMINISTRIVIA

The Center for Disease Control has released a list of symptoms of bird flu. If you experience any of the following, please seek medical treatment immediately:

1. High fever

2. Congestion

3. Nausea

4. Fatigue

5. Aching in the joints

6. An irresistible urge to crap on someone's windshield.

☒

Advert in the British Medical Journal

FOR SALE: Real bone half-skeleton, in better condition than seller. £250.

☒

From a Health Education Authority leaflet on Sexually Transmitted Diseases:
"We don't know why, but it seems that men don't get bacterial vaginosis."

☒

I'm not into working out. My philosophy is no pain, no pain.

☒

The billing clerk called Mrs. Breithart saying, "Mrs. Breithart, your check came back."
She answered, "So did my arthritis."

☒

Getting things done in a hospital is like mating elephants.

It's done at a high level.
It's accomplished with a great
deal of roaring and screaming.
It takes two years to produce results.

☒

A man entered a bus with both of his front pants pockets full of golf balls and sat down next to a blonde.

The blonde kept looking quizzically at him and his bulging pockets.

Finally, after many glances from her, he said, "Golf balls."

The blonde continued to look at him thoughtfully and finally asked, "Does it hurt as much as tennis elbow?"

☒

Five leading causes of death in the US in 1905 were:

Pneumonia and influenza
Tuberculosis
Diarrhea
Heart disease
Stroke

☒

Scientists have discovered a food that diminishes a woman's sex drive by ninety percent.
It's called Wedding Cake.

☒

An apology that appeared recently in The Safety and Health Practitioner:

We would like to apologize to readers for the late arrival of our March issue, which was entitled, 'Flammable Materials: Controlling the Hazard.'

The delay was caused by a fire at the printers.

☒

Seen in the BBC canteen in Manchester: In the interests of hygiene, please use tongues when picking up your baked potatoes.

☒

I will seek and find you.
I shall take you to bed and have my way with you.
I will make you ache, shake, and sweat until you moan and groan.
I will make you beg for mercy, beg for me to stop.
I will exhaust you to the point that you will be relieved when I'm finished with you.
When I am finished with you, you will be weak for days.
I am the Flu – *Who did you think I was?*

☒

Michael Anthony Horne filed a lawsuit against the City of San Antonio for a wrongful arrest last year that cost him the ashes of his grandmother. He had pulled off the road to nap, which looked suspicious to a passing patrolman, who searched Horne's car and found the ashes, which he submitted to a field test, which turned up positive for methamphetamines. Horne was in jail for thirty days until he made bail, and the case has cost him his job, his car, his apartment and his military reserve status. Two subsequent tests of the ashes were negative for drugs, but the tests consumed almost all of the ashes.

☒

What is the difference between Mononucleosis and Herpes?

One can get Mononucleosis from snatching a kiss. . .

☒

In May, the Food and Drug Administration voted 5-to-4 to continue approval of the human skin replacement patches made by Organogenesis Inc. of Canton, Mass. The company's technique is to cultivate and harvest the fastest-growing source of raw material: circumcision residue. One snipped foreskin can eventually produce 200,000 three-inch disks of fake skin. The Economist magazine called this use of foreskin, "The most profitable since David presented Saul with a sack load to gain the throne of Israel.

☒

What does a seventy five year old woman have between her breasts?
Her navel.

☒

A doctor was giving a lesson on the circulation of the blood. Trying to describe it more clearly, he said, "If I stood on my head, the blood, as you know, would run into it, and I would turn red in the face."

"Yes," the audience said."

Then why is it that while I am standing upright in the ordinary position the blood doesn't run into my feet?"

Terrible Tommy answered, "Because your feet aren't empty."

☒

What is a JCAHO auditor?
Someone who arrives after the battle and bayonets all the wounded.

☒

Be careful about reading health books.
You may die of a misprint. - *Mark Twain*

☒

Yesterday, university scientists released the results of a recent analysis that revealed the presence of female hormones in beer. Men should take a concerned look at their beer consumption. The theory is that beer contains female hormones (hops contain phytoestrogens) and that by drinking enough beer, men turn into women.

To test the theory, two hundred men were served and drank twelve bottles of beer each within a one hour period. It was then observed that one hundred percent of the test subjects:

- ☞ Gained weight.
- ☞ Talked excessively without making sense.
- ☞ Became overly emotional.
- ☞ Couldn't drive.
- ☞ Failed to think rationally.
- ☞ Argued over nothing.
- ☞ Had to sit down while urinating.
- ☞ Refused to apologize when obviously wrong.

No further testing was considered necessary.

☒

Have you heard of the new douche made of honey and alum.
Sweeter for the eater and tighter for the peter.

☒

Medical science is so wonderful. Now, after another million dollar study they have found out why women yawn and stretch in the morning.
It is because they have no balls to scratch.

☒

A woman is attending an anatomy class. The subject of the day is involuntary muscle movement. The instructor was hoping to perk up the students a bit and asks the woman if she knows what her asshole does when she has an orgasm.

"Sure," she says, "He's at home taking care of the kids."

☒

Did you hear about the dyslexic that walked into a bra.

☒

Does the name Pavlov ring a bell?

☒

A friend of mine developed a bad back.
So he started to get a little on the side.

☒

There is a difference between a psychopath and a neurotic.
A psychopath thinks two and two are five.
A neurotic knows two and two are four, but he worries about it.

☒

I just read that the IRS Commissioner is to become the new head of the Red Cross. He believes getting blood from people should be no problem.

☒

Did you hear about the Aussie who had a brain transplant?
The brain rejected him a week later.

☒

Five-year-old Becky answered the door when the census taker came by. She told the census taker that her daddy was a doctor and wasn't home, because he was performing an appendectomy.

The census taker said, "That sure is a big word for such a little girl. Do you know what it means?"

"Sure do. Fifteen-hundred bucks, and that doesn't even include the anesthesiologist."

☒

I thought I saw a light at the end of the tunnel, but it was only some bastard with a flashlight bringing me more work.

☒

What do you get when you cross an elephant and a skin doctor?
Pachydermatologist

☒

A lawyer, a cartographer, and a doctor were having a theological debate. Each of them was arguing that God was a member of his profession.

"Remember," said the doctor, "The first thing God did was to bring Adam and Eve into the world. He must be a doctor."

The cartographer said, "Before God created Adam and Eve, He separated the seas from the land and brought order out of chaos. He must be a cartographer."

The lawyer stood up and asked, "Who do you think created the chaos?"

☒

The problem with the gene pool is that there is no lifeguard.

☒

A man was telling his friend, "I just bought a new hearing aid. It cost me four thousand dollars, but it is state of the art."

"Really?" answered the neighbor. "What kind is it?"

"Twelve o'clock."

☒

What is a seizure?
A Roman emperor.

☒

Proverb: Man who eat many prunes get good run for money.

☒

A brain is as strong as its weakest think.

☒

Impotence: Nature's way of saying 'no hard feelings'.

☒

Name a disease associated with cigarettes.
Premature death.

☒

What is artificial insemination?
When the farmer does it to the bull instead of the cow.

☒

There are more bacteria in your mouth than there are people in the world.

☒

How many managed care reviewers does it take to change a light bulb?

Five.

One to receive the authorization forms and put them at the bottom of a pile;

The second to put the pile in a storage closet;

The third to refuse to authorize the light bulb change because the authorization forms were never received;

The fourth to process the resubmitted authorization forms; and

The fifth to authorize a ten-watt light bulb because it uses less electricity.

☒

Reading while sunbathing makes you well red.

☒

MEDICAL INTEGRITY

A large hospital planned to buy up a number of physician medical practices. As their existing legal staff was already quite busy dealing with lawsuits, the hospital decided to hire a new lawyer to handle the contracts with the medical practices.

The astute hospital administrator decided he would interview some young lawyers.

"I am sure that you are aware that our hospital has acquired a considerable reputation regarding the integrity of its dealings with our physicians," the administrator began with one of the first applicants. He continued, "We require that special person whose integrity matches that of our venerable institution."

He leaned close to the young lawyer, "Mr. Obromowitz, are you an honest lawyer?"

"Honest?" replied the young applicant, "My life is the definition of the word honesty. Why, I'm so honest that my parents lent me thirty thousand dollars for law school and I paid back every last cent the minute I tried my very first case."

"I'm impressed. What sort of case was it?"

The lawyer looked down at his shoes and admitted, "They sued me for the money."

The administrator smiled and said, "You'll fit right in here. You're hired."

TOP TEN BAD HMO SIGNS

10.Your annual breast exam is done at Hooters.

9. Directions to your doctor's office include, "Take a left when you enter the trailer park."

8. The tongue depressor tastes faintly of Fudgsicles.

7. The only proctologist in the plan is "Gus" from Roto-Rooter.

6. The only item listed under Preventive Care coverage is "An apple a day."

5. Your primary care physician is wearing the pants you gave to Goodwill last month.

4. 'The patient is responsible for 200% of out-of-network charges' is not a typo.

3. The only one hundred percent expense covered is embalming.

2. With your last HMO your Prozac didn't come in different colors with little "M"s on them.

1. You ask for Viagra; you get a Popsicle stick and duct tape.

HEALTHCARE POLITICS

When a panel of doctors was asked to vote on adding a new wing to their hospital, the Allergists voted to scratch it and the Dermatologists advised no rash moves.

The Gastroenterologists had a gut feeling about it, but the Neurologists thought the administration had a lot of nerve, and the Obstetricians stated they were all laboring under a misconception.

The Ophthalmologists considered the idea shortsighted. The Pathologists yelled, “Over my dead body,” while the Pediatricians said, “Grow up.”

The Psychiatrists thought the whole idea was madness. The surgeons decided to wash their hands of the whole thing and the Radiologists could see right through it.

The physicians thought it was a bitter pill to swallow and the Plastic Surgeons said, “This puts a whole new face on the matter.”

The Podiatrists thought it was a step forward, but the Urologists felt the scheme wouldn’t hold water.

The Anesthesiologists thought the whole idea was a gas and the Cardiologists didn’t have the heart to say no.

In the end, the Proctologists decided to leave the decision up to some asshole in administration.

CUTBACKS

In an effort to reduce costs this year, the following are effective immediately. Please share this information with your patients and physicians as soon as possible.

1. Food service will be discontinued immediately. Patients wishing to eat will want to get their families to bring them a brown bag meal, or you may make your own arrangements with Subway, Dominoes, etc. Coin-operated telephones will be available in the patient rooms for this purpose.

2. Our PBX operators have all been let go, so if your are walking through the lobby and hear the telephone ringing, please answer it.

3. We have found it necessary to make substantial reductions in our transport team so we ask the cooperation of all patients. One transporter will take at least six patients in wheelchairs at a time to Radiology, PT and other services. Please form a "train" by holding tightly on to the handles of the wheelchair in front of you.

4. Our Emergency Room is really busy from 3 PM to 11 PM so, if you can, please have your accidents and heart attacks in the mornings or early afternoons. That would really be helpful and will help to reduce your wait.

5. To expedite surgery cases, all AM admits and outpatient surgery patients are asked to report to the hospital three hours prior to surgery. Go to Central Sterile and pick up a clean instrument tray and surgery pack and proceed to the Surgery Holding area. To help us reduce drug costs, please take several Aleve prior to arriving at the hospital for surgery.

6. Patients anticipating the need for a bedpan can check one out in the gift shop. They will be available in a wide variety of colors and styles to meet the aesthetic and physical requirements of our patients. A deposit will be required but is fully refundable if bedpans are returned clean.

7. To reduce patients' lengths of stay, nurses will have a choice of using in-line skates or skateboards. To expedite response to patient's needs and discharges, nurse call systems will be modified and will be wired to a collar worn by nurses, which will deliver a mild shock when pushed by the patient.

8. Taking a cue from the airlines, Respiratory Therapists will be replaced by oxygen masks which will, should the need arise, automatically drop from the ceiling over patient beds. If this occurs, please place the mask over your nose and mouth and breathe normally.

9. The hospital got a real sweet deal on surplus white waiters' jackets and these will be issued to all physicians. Doctors, we apologize in advance because the jackets already had a first name embroidered on the pocket. We will work with you to find a name that you can live with. If you also are on the staff at the University Hospital, we hope this won't be a problem. We recognize that in academic settings, 'length of coat status' is very important.

10. All first time moms are asked to volunteer to help out on the Pediatrics floor - not only will this reduce hospital costs, but it will give you a much needed experience and a dose of reality after ogling over your own precious sleeping bundle of joy.

11. Housekeeping and physical therapy are being combined. Mops will be issued to those patients who are ambulatory, thus providing range-of-motion exercises as well as a clean environment.

Family members and friends of patients and ambulatory patients may also sign up to clean public areas to receive special discounts on their final bills. Time cards will be provided.

12. Plant operations and Engineering are being eliminated. The hospital has subscribed to the TIME-LIFE "How to..." series of maintenance books. These books can be checked out from administration and a toolbox will be standard equipment on all nursing units. We will be receiving the series at a rate of one volume every other month. We already have the volume on Basic Wiring, but if a non-electrical problem occurs, please try to handle it as best as you can until the appropriate volume arrives.

13. Cutbacks in the phlebotomy staff will be accommodated by only performing blood-related lab tests on patients who are already bleeding.

14. Physicians will be informed that they may order no more than two x-rays per patient stay. This is due to the turnaround time required by Walgreen's photo lab. Two prints will be provided for the price of one, and physicians are being advised to clip coupons from the Sunday paper if they want extra sets. Walgreen's will honor all competitors' coupons for one-hour processing in emergency situations.

15. In light of the extremely hot summer temperature and the high A/C bills that we received last summer, out new policy is to have fans available for sale or lease in the hospital gift shop. For those patients who do not wish to use electric fans, the old reliable hand held cardboard fans on a stick are free upon request.

16. The cost of hospital gowns continues to escalate so patients are asked to bring their own pajama top, which nurses will be happy to slit up the back for you. Pajama bottoms are not permitted on patient units.

MEDICAL HEADLINES

Iraqi Head Seeks Arms

Is There a Ring of Debris around Uranus?

Panda Mating Fails; Veterinarian Takes Over

Miners Refuse to Work after Death

Typhoon Rips through Cemetery; Hundreds Dead

Man Struck by Lightning Faces Battery Charge

New Study of Obesity Looks for Larger Test Group

Astronaut Takes Blame for Gas in Spacecraft

Kids Make Nutritious Snacks

Hospitals Sued by 7 Foot Doctors

ASYLUM

A doctor from the asylum decided to take his patients to a baseball game. For weeks in advance, he coached his patients to respond to his commands. When the day of the game arrived, everything seemed to be going well.

As the national anthem started, the doctor yelled, “Up nuts.”

And the patients complied by standing up. After the anthem he yelled, “Down nuts.” And they all sat.

After a home run he yelled, “Cheer nuts.” And they all broke into applause and cheers.

Thinking things were going very well; he decided to go get a beer and a hot dog, leaving his assistant in charge.

When he returned there was a riot in progress. Finding his assistant, he asked what happened.

The assistant replied, “Everything was fine until a vendor walked by and yelled, ‘Peanuts’.”

MEDICAL RECORDS

The following is purportedly a collection of errors found on hospital patient medical records in one hospital.

The lab test indicated abnormal lover function.

The baby was delivered, the cord clamped and cut, and handed to the pediatrician, who breathed and cried immediately.

Exam of genitalia reveals that he is circus sized.

The skin was moist and dry.

She stated that she had been constipated for most of her life until 1989 when she got a divorce.

The patient was in his usual state of good health until his airplane ran out of gas and crashed.

I saw your patient today, who is still under our car for physical therapy.

Patient was alert and unresponsive.

When she fainted, her eyes rolled around the room.

Bleeding started in the rectal area and continued all the way to Los Angeles.

Both breasts are equal and reactive to light and accommodation.

She is numb from her toes down.

While in the emergency room, she was examined, x-rated and sent home.

The patient was to have a bowel resection. However, he took a job as a stockbroker instead.

The patient suffers from occasional, constant, infrequent headaches.

ADVANCED HEALTHCARE

A Japanese doctor says, “Medicine in my country is so far advanced that we can take a kidney out of one man, put it in another man, and have him out looking for work in six weeks.”

A German doctor replies, “That is nothing. We can take a lung out of one person, put it in another, and have him out looking for work in four weeks.”

A British doctor says, “In my country medicine is so advanced that we can take half a heart out of one person, put it in another, and have both of them out looking for work in two weeks.”

The Canadian doctor, not to be outdone, says, “You guys are way behind. We took a woman with no brains, and sent her to Michigan, where she became Governor, and half the state is out looking for work.”

FACE LIFT

A middle-aged woman decides to have a face lift for her birthday. She spends five thousand dollars and feels pretty good about the results.

On her way home, she stops at a newsstand to buy a newspaper. Before leaving she says to the clerk, “I hope you don’t mind my asking, but how old do you think I am?”

“About thirty-two,” was the reply. “I’m exactly forty-seven,” the woman says.

A little while later she goes into McDonald’s and asks the counter girl the very same question. She replies, “I guess about twenty-nine.”

The woman says, “I’m forty-seven.”

Now she’s feeling really good, stops in a drugstore, and goes up to the counter to get some mints and asks the clerk this burning question.

The clerk responds, “Oh, I would say thirty.”

She proudly responds, “I am forty-seven, but thank you.”

While waiting for the bus to go home, she asks an old man the same question. He replies, “Lady, I am seventy-eight and my eyesight is going. Although, when I was young, there was a sure way to tell how old a woman was, but it requires you to let me put my hands under your bra. Then I can tell you exactly how old you are.”

They waited in silence on the empty street until curiosity got the best of her. She finally replies, “Oh well, go ahead.” He slips both his hands under her blouse and under her bra and begins to feel around very slowly and carefully. After a couple of minutes of this, she says, “Okay, how old am I?” He completes one last squeeze of her breasts and says, “Madam, you are forty-seven.”

The amazed woman says, “That was incredible, how did you know?”

The old man replies, “I was behind you in line at McDonald’s.”

PHONE USAGE

Distinguishing Paranoid Schizophrenia from a normal cell phone user

Social Distance: The individual with schizophrenia will generally retreat to a considerate distance from others when he needs to converse with his voices.

The cell phone user will stand right next to you, talk in a loud voice, and gesticulate in your face.

Safe Driving Technique: The individual with schizophrenia does not need to dial, and thus is a much safer driver.

The cell phone user often needs to look at his phone to dial while driving, causing him to drive over yellow lines and endanger others on the road.

Restaurants: The individual with schizophrenia is less likely to be noticed because he usually has his conversations in eateries where the ambient noise drowns out his conversation.

The cell phone user is more likely to be talking loudly in a quiet, expensive restaurant.

Prognosis: Individuals with schizophrenia often seek help for their difficulties, and are quite responsive to treatment.

Cell phone users are remarkable for their lack of insight and resistance to any form of social, medical, or legal intervention.

ARTHRITIS

A drunken man, who smelled like beer, sat down on a subway seat next to a priest.

The man's tie was stained, his face was plastered with red lipstick, and a half empty bottle of gin was sticking out of his torn coat pocket. He opened his newspaper and began reading.

After a few minutes the man turned to the priest and asked, "Tell me, father, what causes arthritis?"

"My son, it's caused by loose living, being with cheap, wicked women, too much alcohol, and contempt for your fellow man, sleeping around with prostitutes and lack of bath."

"Well, I'll be damned," the drunk muttered, returning to his paper.

The priest is thinking about what he had said and nudged the man and apologized. "I'm very sorry. I didn't mean to come on so strong. How long have you had arthritis?"

"I don't have it, father. I was just reading here that the Pope does."

SIGNS

At Gynecologist's Office **Dr. Jones - at your cervix**
At a Proctologist's door **To expedite your visit please back in**
On a Plastic Surgeon's Office door **Hello - Can we pick your nose**
In a Nonsmoking Area **If we see smoke -** **We will assume you are on fire and take appropriate action**
On a Maternity Room door **Push Push Push**
At an Optometrist's Office **If you don't see what you're looking for** **you've come to the right place**
In a Veterinarian's waiting room **Be back in 5 minutes - Sit - Stay**
In a Podiatrist's office **Time wounds all heels**

OUR DIET

A doctor was addressing a large audience in Tampa. The material we put into our stomachs is enough to have killed most of us sitting here, years ago.

Red meat is awful. Soft drinks corrode your stomach lining. Chinese food is loaded with MSG. High fat diets can be disastrous, and none of us realizes the long-term harm caused by the germs in our drinking water.

There is one thing that is the most dangerous of all, and most of us have, or will, eat it.

Can anyone here tell me what food it is that causes the most grief and suffering for years after eating it?

After several seconds of quiet, a seventy-five year old man in the front row, raised his hand and said, "Wedding cake."

WHY CLONING IS BAD

Harder than ever to land a role in those new Wrigley's commercials featuring the Doublemint Octuplets.

Two words: Gilbert Gottfried

Any scientific advancement that stems from the result of Scottish people doing strange things to sheep is bound to have dire consequences.

In mere weeks, Bill Gates (v1.0, v1.2, v2.0, v3.0, v3.1 & v5.0) has all the money on the entire planet.

If you think there are too many idiots shouting "Show me the money!" on every occasion now, just wait.

Rush Limbaugh takes his self-affection to a whole new level, and suddenly is in favor of same-sex marriages.

"Penn & Penn & Teller & Teller & Teller & Penn & Penn & Teller & Penn" much harder to fit on comedy club marquee.

And you think it's hard to find your size now!

And the final score: the New York Gretzkys - 408, the Pittsburgh Lemieuxs -99.

"Ladies & Gentlemen: The John Tesh Philharmonic Orchestra!"

Seventeen Mark Fuhrmans, and suddenly OJ's defense doesn't seem quite as far-fetched.

DICTATIONS

The following quotes were supposedly taken from actual medical records as dictated by physicians.

I have suggested that he loosen his pants before standing, and then, when he stands with the help of his wife, they should fall to the floor.

She slipped on the ice and apparently her legs went in separate directions in early December.

The patient experienced sudden onset of severe shortness of breath with a picture of acute pulmonary edema at home while having sex which gradually deteriorated in the emergency room.

Between you and me, we ought to be able to get this lady pregnant.

Since she can't get pregnant with her husband, I thought you would like to work her up.

Coming from Detroit, this man has no children.

SPECIMEN ROBBERY

Excerpted from an article which appeared in the Dublin Times.

Once inside the bank shortly after midnight, their efforts at disabling the security system got underway immediately.

The robbers, who expected to find one or two large safes filled with cash and valuables, were surprised to see hundreds of smaller safes throughout the bank.

The robbers cracked the first safe's combination, and inside they found only a small bowl of Vanilla pudding. As recorded on the bank's audio tape system, one robber said, "At least we'll have a bit to eat."

The robbers opened up a second safe, and it also contained nothing but vanilla pudding. The process continued until all safes were opened. They did not find one pound Sterling, a diamond, or an ounce of gold.

Instead, all the safes contained covered bowls of pudding. The disappointed robbers made a quiet exit. They each left with nothing more than a queasy, uncomfortably full stomach.

The next day's newspaper headline read:
IRELAND'S LARGEST SPERM BANK ROBBED EARLY THIS MORNING

CLONE

A rich and famous professor decided that he was just too smart to die and leave the world alone without him.

He locked himself in his laboratory for months and finally perfected a method to make a clone of himself. The clone came out perfect and was identical in every detail to the original.

The professor was excited at his success and embarked on a worldwide lecture tour. After a time the clone became the alter ego of the professor and when he would sit on the stage behind him he would always make obscene gestures and cuss and swear at the professor.

Finally, this became too much for the professor to take as he was losing speaking engagements, because it appeared that the clone was not his exact copy. He decided that there was no alternative and he would have to do away with the clone.

After one of his lectures in Colorado, he took the clone and went up to the mountains to see the sights. As they were standing on the edge of a cliff, the professor came up behind the clone and pushed him off.

Later that evening at his hotel the police came and arrested the professor.

The charge was, "Making an obscene clone fall."

HEALTH AND WELFARE

The government has just instituted a policy of nationalized medicine which will extend into all areas of health and welfare. This will go so far as to include proxy fathers for women who wish to become mothers, without the benefit of wedlock. A woman can apply for the services of a government agent to fulfill her needs. Miss Green has applied and has been waiting for the agent to arrive for quite some time.

About that time, photographer is in the neighborhood taking baby pictures and stops by Miss Green's house to solicit some business.

He Good morning.

She Good morning to you.

He You probably don't know me but I represent. . .

She Oh, yes. You don't have to explain. I've been expecting you.

He I make a specialty of babies. I especially prefer twins.

She That is what I understand. Please have a seat.

He Has anyone told you about my work?

She Yes, I know all about it. I am ready to get started.

He Well, we may as well start now.

She This is new to me. How do we start?

He Just leave everything to me. I would recommend two in the bathtub and a couple on the floor and possibly one on the couch.

She Tub, couch, floor?

He Well, my dear, even the best of us can't guarantee a good one each time. I am sure, though, that one will turn out from the six.

She This all seems a bit informal.

He No, not at all, in my line some of the best work is done in a hurry. Here, look at some of the shots in this album. Look at this beauty. It took three hours but really turned out well.

She Yes, a lovely child.

He This was a tough assignment. You may not believe it but this was done on the top of a double deck bus.

She My goodness.

He It isn't too bad when a man knows his business. It can even be a real pleasure. There is one I did with one shot through the lady's window. It came out perfect.

She I can hardly believe it.

He And here is a picture of the prettiest twins in town. They turned out rather well considering there mother was so difficult. I had to knock off this job in the park, in the snow. People were crowded all around us.

She My goodness, that must have been a sight.

He It took over four hours but I was lucky enough to have a few friends help me on that job. I could have taken one more shot before dark but the squirrels were trying to nibble at my equipment. Enough talk! If you are ready, I will get my tripod and get started.

She Tripod?

He Yes, I need it to rest my equipment on. It's too heavy for me to hold for any length of time. Miss Green, speak to me. Have you fainted?

MEDICAL HOTLINE

Hello, and welcome to the Mental Health Hotline.

If you are obsessive or compulsive, press 1 repeatedly.

If you are co-dependant, please ask someone to press 2 for you.

If you have multiple personalities, please press 3, 4, 5 and 6.

If you are paranoid, we already know who you are, but stay on the line while we trace your call.

If you are delusional, press 7 and your call will be transferred to the mother ship.

If you are schizophrenic, listen carefully and a small voice will tell you which number to press.

If you have short term memory loss, press 9, if you have short term memory loss, press 9, if you have short term memory loss, press 9.

If you have low self esteem, please hang up. All our operators are too busy to talk to you.

BONUS

The Air Force found they had too many officers and NCOs and decided to offer an early retirement bonus.

They promised any officer who volunteered for retirement a bonus of a thousand dollars for every inch measured in a straight line between any two points in his body.

The officer got to choose what those two points would be.

The first officer, who accepted, asked that he be measured from the top of his head to the tip of his toes. He was measured at six feet and walked out with a bonus of seventy two thousand dollars.

The second officer who accepted was a little smarter and asked to be measured from the tip of his outstretched hands to his toes. He walked out with ninety six thousand dollars.

The third one was a grizzly old Master Sergeant who, when asked where he would like to be measured replied, “from the tip of my penis to my testicles.”

It was suggested by the pension man that he might want to reconsider; explaining about the nice checks the previous two officers had received.

The old Sergeant insisted and they decided to go along with him providing the measurement was taken by a medical officer.

The medical officer arrived and instructed the Sergeant to drop his shorts, which he did.

The medical officer placed the tape measure on the tip of the Sergeant’s penis and began to work back. “My God.” he suddenly exclaimed, “Where are your testicles?”

The old Sergeant calmly replied, “Vietnam.”

MEDICAL STATISTICS

The number of physicians in the US is 700,000.
Accidental deaths caused by Physicians per year are 120,000.
Accidental deaths per physician are 0.171.
(*US Dept. of Health Human Services*)

The number of gun owners in the US is 80,000,000

The number of accidental gun deaths per year (all age groups) is 1,500.

The number of accidental deaths per gun owner is .0000188.

Statistically, doctors are approximately 9,000 times more dangerous than gun owners.

Not everyone has a gun, but almost everyone has at least one doctor.

Please alert your friends to this alarming threat. We must ban doctors before this gets out of hand.

As a public health measure I have withheld the statistics on lawyers for fear that the shock could cause people to seek medical attention.

CHOKING AID

Suddenly, a woman at a nearby table, who is eating a sandwich, begins to cough. After a minute or so, it becomes apparent that she is in real distress.

One of the hillbillies looks at her and says, “Kin ya swaller?”

The woman shakes her head no.

“Kin ya breathe?”

The woman begins to turn blue and shakes her head no.

The hillbilly walks over to the woman, lifts up the back of her dress, yanks down her drawers, and quickly gives her right butt cheek a lick with his tongue.

The woman is so shocked that she has a violent spasm and the obstruction flies out of her mouth.

As she begins to breathe again, the hillbilly walks slowly back to the bar. His partner says, “Ya know, I’d heerd of that there Hind Lick Maneuver, but I ain’t never seed nobody do it.”

ADMINISTRATIVE CUTBACKS

Great moments in paperwork: How to fill out care review forms

1. Make sure you give a complete history of current and past presenting complaints:

The patient has been depressed ever since she began seeing me in 1988. She is tearful and crying constantly. She also appears to be depressed. . She has no past history of suicides.

2. Document whether you are ordering laboratory studies.

Patient has left her white blood cells at her primary care doctor's office.

3. Document discharge condition and planned disposition.

The patient is ready to leave the hospital. She is feeling much better except for her original complaints.

4. Description of a patient fall.

A sudden, often unexplained change in position in which an adult patient comes to rest unintentionally on the floor.

Discharge status: Alive but without permission. The patient will need disposition, and therefore we will get the outpatient psychiatrist to dispose of her."

Insurance

CO PAYS

A sixty-five-year-old couple went to the doctor's office. The doctor asked how he could help. The man said, "Will you watch us have sexual intercourse?" The doctor looked puzzled but agreed. When the couple finished, the doctor said, "There is nothing wrong with the way you have intercourse." He then charged them forty dollars.

This happened several weeks in a row. The couple would make an appointment, have intercourse, pay the doctor, and leave. Finally, the doctor asked, "Just exactly what are you trying to find out?" "We're not trying to find out anything," said the old man. "She is married, and we can't go to her house. I am married so we can't go to my house. Holiday Inn charges sixty bucks. Hilton Hotel charges ninety dollars. We can do it here for forty dollars and I get thirty bucks back from Medicare for a visit to the doctor's office."

$ $ $

The seven-year old girl told her mom, "Terrible Tommy in my class asked me to play doctor."
"Oh, dear," the mother nervously sighed. "What happened, honey?"
"Nothing. He made me wait forty-five minutes, then double-billed the insurance company."

$ $ $

"I just signed up with an insurance company that believes in preventative medicine.

"That sounds great. Why are you so grumpy?"

"It turns out that preventative medicine means their prescription plan prevents me from getting my medicine."

$ $ $

What is the ideal weight of a retrospective claims reviewer?
About three pounds, including the urn.

$ $ $

LENGTH OF STAY

A doctor, a nurse, and the CEO of an HMO all died on the same day.

Upon approaching the Pearly Gates, Saint Peter asked the doctor why he should enter the Pearly Gates.

The doctor answered, “I worked in the Emergency Department and saved many lives during the course of my career.”

Saint Peter agreed that he should be admitted.

Saint Peter asked the nurse why she should be allowed to enter the Pearly Gates.

She replied, “I worked in a hospice and comforted the ill and the dying for many years. I even cared for the families.”

Saint Peter admitted her into heaven as well.

Saint Peter then turned to the CEO of the HMO and asked him the same question.

The CEO responded, “I have cut the cost of health care and prevented many unnecessary procedures.”

Saint Peter thought about that for a minute then said, “I have decided to allow you into heaven, but only for three days.”

IN THE BEGINNING

God populated the earth with broccoli and cauliflower and spinach, green and yellow vegetables of all kinds, so man and woman would live long and healthy lives.

And Satan created McDonald's, and McDonald's brought forth the ninety-nine-cent double cheeseburger.

And Satan said to man, "You want fries with that?"

And man said, "Supersize them." And man gained pounds.

And God created the healthful yogurt, that woman might keep her figure that man found so fair.

And Satan brought forth chocolate. And woman gained pounds.

And God said, "Try my crispy fresh salad."

And Satan brought forth ice cream. And woman gained pounds.

And God said, "I have sent thee heart-healthy vegetables and olive oil with which to cook them."

And Satan brought forth chicken-fried steak so big it needed its own platter. And man gained pounds and his cholesterol level soared skyward.

And God brought forth running shoes so man could lose those extra pounds.

And Satan brought forth cable TV with remote control so man would not have to toil to change channels between ESPN and ESPN2. And man gained pounds.

And God said, "You are running up the score, Devil."

And God brought forth the potato, a vegetable naturally low in fat and brimming with nutrition.

And Satan peeled off the healthful skin and sliced the starchy center into chips and deep-fat fried them, and he created sour cream dip.

And man clutched his remote control and ate the potato chips swaddled in cholesterol.

And Satan saw and said, "It is good."

And man went into cardiac arrest.

And God sighed and created quadruple bypass surgery.

And Satan created HMO's.

THE HMO

Mr. Smith goes to the doctor's office to collect his wife's test results.

The lab tech says to him, "I'm sorry, sir, but there has been a bit of a mix-up and we have a problem. When we sent the samples from your wife to the lab, the samples from another Mrs. Smith were sent as well, and we are now uncertain which one is your wife's. Frankly, it is either bad or terrible!"

"What do you mean?"

"Well, one Mrs. Smith has tested positive for Alzheimer's and the other for AIDS. We can't tell which results are for your wife."

"That's terrible! Can we do the test over?"

"Normally, yes, but you have an HMO. It won't pay for these expensive tests more than once."

"Well, what am I supposed to do now?"

"The HMO recommends that you drop your wife off in the middle of town. If she finds her way home, don't sleep with her."

COURT TRANSCRIPT

Q: Doctor, how many autopsies have you performed on dead people?
All my autopsies are performed on dead people.

Q: Do you recall the time that you examined the body?
The autopsy started around 8:30 p.m.

Q: And Mr. Dennington was dead at the time?
No, he was sitting on the table wondering why I was doing an autopsy.

Q: Are you qualified to give a urine sample?

Q: Doctor, before you performed the autopsy, did you check for a pulse?
No.

Q: Did you check for blood pressure?
No.

Q: Did you check for breathing?
No.

Q: So, then it is possible that the patient was alive when you began the autopsy?
No.

Q: How can you be so sure, doctor?
Because his brain was sitting on my desk in a jar.

Q: But could the patient have still been alive nevertheless?
It is possible that he could have been alive and practicing law somewhere.

HEALTH PLAN

Queen Elizabeth II was visiting one of New York's finest hospitals and during her tour of the wards, she passed a room where one of the male patients was masturbating.

"Oh my goodness," said the Queen. "That's disgraceful, what is the meaning of this?"

The doctor leading the tour explains, "I am sorry your Royal Highness, but this man has a very serious condition where his testicles fill up rapidly with semen. If he doesn't do what he is doing at least five times per day, he could swell up and he might die"

"Oh, I am sorry," said the Queen, "I was unaware that such a medical condition existed."

On the same floor they soon passed another room where a young, blonde nurse was performing oral sex on another patient.

"Oh my God," said the Queen, "What's happening here?"

The doctor replied, "Same problem, better health plan."

HMO Q & A

Q. *What does HMO stand for?*
A. This is actually a variation of the phrase, 'Hey, Moe' Its roots go back to a concept pioneered by Dr. Moe Howard of 'The Three Stooges,' who discovered that a patient could be made to forget about the pain in his foot if he was poked hard enough in the eyes.

Q. *I just joined an HMO. How difficult will it be to choose the doctor I want?*
A. Slightly more difficult than choosing your parents. Your insurer will provide you with a book listing all the doctors who are participating in the plan. These doctors fall into two categories those who are no longer accepting new patients, and those who will see you but are no longer part of the plan.

Q. *Do all diagnostic procedures require pre-certification?*
A. No. Only those you need.

Q. *What are preexisting conditions?*
A. This is a term used by the grammatically challenged when they want to talk about existing conditions. Unfortunately, we appear to be pre-stuck with 'pre and now' meaning the same.

Q. *Can I get coverage for my preexisting conditions?*
A. Certainly, as long as they don't require any treatment.

Q. *What happens if I want to try alternative forms of medicine?*
A. You will need to find alternative forms of payment.

Q. *My pharmacy plan only covers generic drugs, but I need the name brand. I tried the generic medication, but it gave me a stomach ache. What should I do?*
A. See above. Poke yourself in the eye.

Q. *What if I'm away from home and I get sick?*
A. You really shouldn't do that.

Q. *Will health care be any different in the next century?*
A. Probably not, but if you call right now, you might get an appointment by then.

CHEAP HEALING NOT WORKING

Excerpt: Prayer didn't help sick - by Jeremy Manier, Chicago Tribune, 2006

CHICAGO - Praying for a sick heart patient may feel right to people of faith, but it doesn't appear to improve the patient's health, according to a new study that is the largest ever done on the healing powers of prayer.

Indeed, researchers at the Harvard Medical School and five other US medical centers found, to their bewilderment, that coronary-bypass patients who knew strangers were praying for them fared significantly worse than people who got no prayers. The team speculated that telling patients about the prayers may have caused "performance anxiety," or perhaps a fear that doctors expected the worst.

"Obviously, my colleagues were surprised by the unexpected and counterintuitive outcome," said the Rev. Dean Marek, director of chaplain services at the Mayo Clinic in Rochester, Minn., and a study co-investigator.

It was a strange end for the mammoth prayer study, which cost $2.4 million and enrolled 1,802 patients who had bypass surgery. Most of the funding came from the British-based John Templeton Foundation, which supports research at the intersection of science and religion.

Previous studies had examined the power of prayer for medical patients, with mixed results. Most did not have the statistical power to reliably detect the effects of prayer, if it had an effect.

The new study, which appears in the April issue of the American Heart Journal, was designed to be large enough to see if patients who knew they were being prayed for had better recoveries.

There was virtually no difference in complication rates between patients in the first two groups. But the third group, in which patients knew they were receiving prayers, had a complication rate of 59 percent, significantly more than the 52 percent in the no-prayer group.

Researchers were at a loss to explain the worsened outcomes in their study.

Medical Definitions

MINI MEDICAL DICTIONARY

Acupuncture	Jab well done
Addiction	Strong weakness
Amnesia	Condition that enables a woman who has gone through labor to have sex again
Anatomy	Something that everyone has but it looks better on a woman
Anus	Latin term for yearly
Arachnoleptic fit	Frantic dance performed just after you've accidentally walked through a spider web
Artery	Study of paintings
Arthritis	Twinges in the hinges
Artificial insemination	When the farmer does it to the bull instead of the cow
Asphalt	What a Proctologist treats
Bacteria	The back door of a cafeteria
Bandages	The Rolling Stones
Barium	What you do with dead folks
Barium	What you do when C.P.R. fails
Benign	What you be after you be eight
Birth control	Avoiding pregnancy through such tactics as swallowing special pills, inserting a diaphragm, using a condom, and dating repulsive men
Bowel	A letter like a, e, i, o or u
Broken Nose	Bent scent instrument

Buck Teeth	Cheap at twice the price
Carcinoma	A valley in California, notable for its heavy smog
Cardiology	Advanced study of poker playing
Cat scan	Searching for the cat
Cauterize	Made eye contact with her
Cesarean Section	Neighborhood in Rome
Clitoris	Type of flower
Coitus	Musical instrument
Colic	Sheep dog
Coma	Punctuation mark used in writing sentences
Condom	Large apartment complex
Congenital	Friendly
Copulation	Refers to how many people live in an area.
Costomer Service	Expensive maintenance fees paid for the privilege of navigating several layers of a vendor's organization to find the answer you are looking for
Cunnilingus	Person that can speak many languages
Cyst	Help your neighbor
D & C	Where the White House is
Darth Vendor	Vendor whose product is so destructive and invasive that it takes over your organization and fills you with a pervasive sense of doom
Death	A grave mistake
Defeat	At de end of de legs
Diagnostic Related Gripes	Oh, my back! Oh, my head!

Diagnostic Related Gropes	Upcoding by any other name
Diaphragm	A drawing in geometry
Diet	That which is put off while you are putting it on. Also penalty for exceeding the feed limit.
Diet	Craving to exclude
Diet	Food that makes other people lose weight
Dilate	To live a long time
Dildo	Variety of sweet pickle
Doctor	Person who kills your ills with pills, and kills you with his bills.
Drug	Chemical which heals a sick body, or a chemical which harms a healthy body.
Drug	A substance that, when injected into a rat, produces a scientific paper
Ecnalubma	Rescue vehicle which can only be seen in the rearview mirror
Egotist	Someone who is usually me-deep in conversation.
Enema	Not a friend
ER	The things on your head that you hear with
Erection	When Japanese people vote
Exercise	To walk up and down a mall, occasionally resting to make a purchase
Eyedropper	Clumsy ophthalmologist
Fallopian Tube	Part of an old fashioned television
Family Planning	The art of spacing your children the proper distance apart to keep you from the edge of financial disaster.

Father	A banker provided by nature
Fester	Quicker
Fetus	Character on Gunsmoke
Fibula	A small lie
Flatulence	Female - An embarrassing byproduct of digestion Male - A source of entertainment, self-expression
Flatulence	The emergency vehicle that picks you up after you are run over by a steamroller
Genes	Blue denim slacks
Genitals	Not Jewish
GI Series	Soldier ball game
Grippe	An old fashioned suitcase
G-String	Part of a fiddle
Hangnail	Coat hook in the waiting room
Hangnail	Coat hook
HAPII	What health care organizations aren't about HIPAA
Head Nurse	Nurse with dirty knees
Hearth Care Organization	National Brotherhood of Chimney Sweeps
Hemmorrhoid	A male from outer space
Herpes	What women do in the Ladies Room
Hipatitis	Terminal coolness
Hormones	What a prostitute does when she doesn't get paid
Hypochondriac	Pill collector
ICU	Peek-a-boo

Impotence	Nature's way of saying, 'no hard feelings'
Impotent	Distinguished, well known
Impregnable	A woman whose memory of labor is still vivid
Incontinent	Where the English spend their vacations
Inoculatte	To take coffee intravenously when you are running late
Integrated Delivery Notwork	So many mergers, so little time, so many failures
Integration Brokee	One who pays those amazing integration fees
Kotex	A radio station out West
Labor pain	Getting hurt at work
Lesbian	Person from the Middle East
Lymph	To walk with a lisp
Masturbate	Used to catch large fish
Maulpractice	What lawyers do to physicians
Medical Staff	Doctor's cane
Menstrual Cycle	Has three wheels
Minor Operation	Digging for coal
Mirth Control	Anything technological or contractual that, when applied or practiced, prevents or discourages the ability to reproduce a sense of humor
Morbid	Higher offer
Mortality	The birth of death
Murketing	Art of confusing the market and your organization simultaneously

Neurosis	Perpetual emotion
Neurotic	Self taught person. Also, a person in a clash by himself.
Nitrates	Cheaper than day rates
Node	All that the doctor understood
Nose	The scenter of your face
Obesity	Bad Breadth
Organic	Kind of music played in a church
Orgasm	Person who accompanies a church choir
OSHA	Protective coating made by half-baking a mixture of fine print, red tape, split hairs, and baloney. Applied at random with a shotgun.
Outpatient	Person who has fainted
Overweight	Something that just sort of snacks up on you
Pap smear	Fatherhood test
Paradox	Two physicians
Paralyze	Two far-fetched stories
Parasites	What you see from the top of the Eiffel Tower
Pathological	A reasonable way to go
Pathology	Study of trails
Patience Accounting	What providers do with proprietary legacy patient accounting systems that have high claims denial rates
Pelvis	Cousin of Elvis
Pharmacist	Helper on the farm
Physician Order Entry	Previously known as Nurse Betty

Physicians Disk Reference	Hottest tunes as picked by your physicians
Polaroid	Eskimo hemorrhoid
Pornography	Business of making records
Post Operative	Military mail man
Practical Nurse	One who marries her rich patient
Pre-dismissive Certification	Early warning from an insurance company that you won't be covered
Pregnancy	Woman in bloom by a man's handiwork
Pregnant	Mislaid woman
Prenatal	When your life was still somewhat your own
Protein	Very tolerant of young people
Psychiatrist	A person who tries to figure out whether an infant in infancy has more fun than an adult in adultery. Also, Person who turns the individual insight out.
Psychic	Someone who can predict the future, but you will still need to make an appointment to see him.
Psychologist	Man who watches everyone else when a beautiful girl enters the room.
Psychotherapy Insight	New truth about a person that he already knew without the words.
Pubic Hair	Wild rabbit
Recovery room	Place to do upholstery
Rectitude	Formal, dignified demeanor assumed by a proctologist immediately before he or she examines you
Rectum	What happened when he was in a bad accident

Reference Information Mogul	Bump on the path to clinical standards
Rheumatic	Amorous
Rubberneck	What you do to relax your wife or girlfriend
Saline	What you do on your friend's boat
Sanitary belt	Drink from a clean glass.
Scale	Thing that registers ten pounds more in a doctor's office than it does at home.
Scientist	One who sees patterns in chaos
Secretion	Tendency to hide things
Seizure	Roman Emperor
Semen	Another term for sailors
Serology	The study of English Knighthood
Silicon	Good for memory, bad for mammary
Silicon Treatment	The bust that money can buy
Skeleton	Bunch of bones with the person scraped off
Smelling Salts	Sailors with B. O.
Sodomy	Special land of fast growing grass
Spread Eagle	An extinct bird
Sterilize	What you do to your first baby's pacifier by boiling it and to your last baby's pacifier by blowing on it.
Sudafed	Brought litigation against a government official
Tablet	Small table
Terminal Illness	Getting sick at the airport

Testicle	Humorous question on an exam
Testicles	What an octopus has eight of
Tibia	Country in North Africa
Toothache	Pain that drives you to extraction.
Tumor	An extra pair
Umbilical Cord	Part of a parachute
Uranus	Greeks favorite planet
Urinate	If you had boobs, you'd be a ten
Urine	Belongs to you. Also, opposite of you're out.
Vaccination	An ouch of prevention
Vagina	Medical term used to describe a heart attack
Varicose	Near by
Vegetarian	Indian word for 'lousy hunter'
Vein	Conceited
Vulva	Automobile made in Sweden
Willy-nilly	Impotent
Wrinkles	What other people have. You have character lines
X-rayed	For adult viewing only
Yawn	Honest opinion openly expressed and the only time some married men ever get to open their mouth.

DOCTOR'S NAMES

Dr. Aikenhead	Allergy specialist
John Bagwell	Anesthesiologist
Dr. Knapp	Anesthesiologist
Dr. D. V. Mallett	Chiropractor
J.A.W. Dobson	Dentist
Philip McCavity	Dentist
Dr. Michelle Moller	Dentist
Lance Boyle	Dermatologist
Dr. Enemau	Gastroenterologist
Dr. Howard Hertz	General Practitioner
Dr. Kwak	General Practitioner
Dr. Palmer	Hand surgeon
Dr. Ake	Internal Medicine
Rita Book	Medical librarian
Paul Bering	Mortician
Diane Berry	Mortician
Dr. Russell Brain	Neurologist
Dr. Sherwood B. Fein	ob/gyn
Dr. Groth	Oncologist
Dr. Bonebreak	Orthopedic Surgeon
Joseph C. Babey	Pediatrician
Dr. John E. Foote	Podiatrist
Dr. Korn	Podiatrist
Dr. Bjerk	Psychiatrist
Dr. Dement	Psychiatrist
Dr. Albright	Radiologist
Dr. Breidin	Respiratory specialist
Dr. D'Eath	Surgeon
Dr. Kutteroff	Surgeon
Ben E. Fischel	Therapist
Dr. Dick Finder	Urologist
Dr. Barksdale	Veterinarian

TAXONOMY OF MEDICAL PROFESSIONS

An acher of bacteriologists

A canker of dentists

A murmur of cardiologists

A stain of cytotechnologists

A rash of dermatologists

A speck of forensic pathologists

A poke of gynecologists

A vessel of heart surgeons

A clot of hematologists

A nursery of obstetricians

A dose of pharmacists

A pile of proctologists

A stream of urologists

Doctors' Secret Handshakes:

Cardiologist	Left hand on your wrist, feeling pulse
Dermatologist	Wears latex glove
Gynecologist	Index and middle fingers extended
Pediatrician	Thumb extended
Psychiatrist	Grasps his own hand

Medical Benefits of Laughter

Laughter is an orgasm triggered by the intercourse of sense and nonsense.

Laughter is good for the soul, good for the heart, and good for the brain.

Anatomically considered, laughing is the sensation of feeling good all over, and showing it principally in one spot.

Laughter is like inner jogging.

We are all born with a backbone, but we have to develop our own funnybone.

Humor is by far the most significant activity of the human brain.

Laughter is a tranquilizer with no side effects. *Arnold Glasgow*

Always laugh when you can. It is cheap medicine. *Lord Byron*

Our five senses are incomplete without the sixth - a sense of humor.

Laughter on the lips hides bulges on the hips.

The art of medicine consists of amusing the patient while nature cures the disease. *Voltaire*

Psychological studies have shown that during an initial contact, it's psychologically impossible to dislike someone who has made you laugh genuinely for five times or more.

Endorphins (pain killers) are released during a deep laugh and Cortisol (Stress hormone) is decreased during laughter.

Statistics showed that 82% of women consistently rank humor as one of the top three qualities of men they want to date.

If you are too busy to laugh, you are too busy.

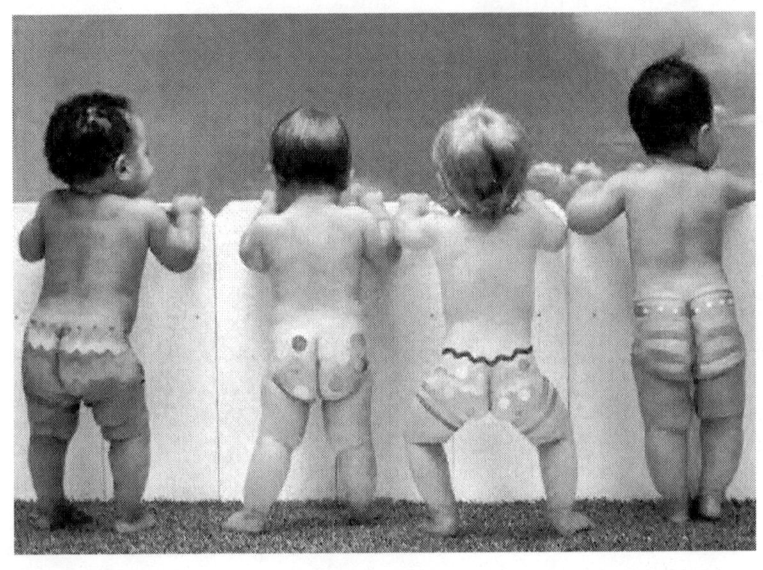

The End

Made in the USA
Lexington, KY
06 December 2010